Discourse on
Transforming Inner Nature

D1719876

Discourse on Transforming Inner Nature

化性谈

Hua Xing Tan

by Wang Fengyi 王凤仪

Translated by Johan Hausen and Jonas Todd Akers
Foreword by Daoist Renunciate Xing De

Valley Spirit Arts
Phoenix, Arizona

Disclaimer
We have exercised due diligence in the translation of the scripture *Discourse on Transforming Inner Nature* and take full responsibility for any inaccuracies, errors and omissions. To the best of our knowledge, the cover image and biography photo of Wang Fengyi are public domain (王凤仪嘉言录 "Information Sharing Web").

Note: The pinyin Romanization system of the People's Republic of China is adopted throughout the book, despite many terms being familiar to the general public from other systems such as the Wade-Giles. Readers should take note that the spelling of "Tao," "Kungfu" and "Chi" are rendered "Dao," "Gongfu" and "Qi." The authors apologize for any possible decrease and diminishing of readers' recognition due to their choice in spelling system. The Five Elements of Wood, Fire, Earth, Metal and Water are capitalized throughout this translation, as they depict wider concepts in Chinese Medicine and Daoism. When the treatise refers to "fire," "water," and so on in the most common sense as physical matter, they are kept lowercase. Any terms that comprise more deeper meanings than the translators could possibly have done justice by choosing a single word are capitalized to invite readers to do their own research. These terms are often, but not exclusively, borrowed from the religious domain.

Library of Congress Control Number: 2017952414
ISBN-13: 978-1-9745-5061-6

Illustrations by "Horiga"
Holger Mauersberger (www.horiga.com)

Coverdesign: Hermitage Design Solutions
(hermitagedesignsolutions@gmail.com)

Photograph of Xing De (Li Shifu) by Jan Valentini

Published by Valley Spirit Arts, LLC (www.valleyspiritarts.com)

I dedicate this work to the creators of the seed of my first life,

my beloved parents Toni and Peter Hausen,

who made great sacrifices to nurture and foster me;

and

to the bestower of my second life, Li Shifu,

who enabled me to open my thoughts.

—Johan Hausen

I would like to dedicate my efforts in this translation to my
cousin Joshua Harris, a truly loving father and husband.
To my Grandmother, Patricia McGill, who was a great and
dear friend. To my family who made me, my many beloved
friends who shaped me, my teachers who showed me the way
and, most importantly, I dedicate this to my wife,
Samantha Akers. You are absolutely the best.
Thank you for seeing me for who I am, standing by me
and helping me see clearly so that I could transform.

—Jonas Akers

师傅领进门，
修行在个人。

The master leads you to enter the gate,
but the cultivation rests on the individual.

—Chinese Proverb

Acknowledgments

Throughout the last two years during which this book took shape, numerous people provided crucial support.

Dr. Henry McCann, Lorraine Wilcox, Leo Tok and Sabine Wilms assisted us with their unrivaled scholarly views on the translation.

Aunty Tahne Harris, Matt Williams, Yue Chen, Ash Ahmed, Carolina LaForesta, and Josh McKenzie contributed invaluable editorial advice.

Lindsey Wei encouraged us with her feedback and review of the treatise to forge ahead.

Emilio and Jan Valentini's creativity made possible the design of this book's cover.

James Manning excelled in the translation excerpts of the *Forty-Nine Barrier* scripture.

Sara Faustino was an indispensable cog in the wheel to liaise with Li Shifu for the calligraphy art.

We also want to express our gratitude to Holger Mauersberger, who did not shun any effort to provide the drawings despite running a busy tattoo studio.

Furthermore we are indebted to Loan Guylaine Tran Trung for translating the preface from French into English.

Last but not least we are thankful to Stuart Alve Olson and Patrick Gross from Valley Spirit Arts for guiding us through all the necessary steps of publishing this book.

放下名利榮辱、

放下喜怒哀愁、

放下執著 分辨、

放下邏輯思考、

放下陰陽凡聖、

讓陽光進來，衝洗自己的過去、

有瞬空霹靂撕裂幻化的蛹衣。

丙申年仲冬 代當白馬山王僊觀吳綿

放下名利荣辱。
放下喜怒哀愁。
放下执箸认知。
放下逻辑控制。
放下阴阳凡圣。
请阳光进来冲刷自己。
有晴空霹雳。
撕裂幻化而蛹衣。

丙申年仲冬武当白马山五仙庙兴德

Put down fame and gain, honor and disgrace.
Put down joy, anger, sorrow, and worry.
Put down attachments and recognition.
Put down logic and confinements.
Put down Yin and Yang, the commoners and the sages.
Request the Yang Radiance to enter in order to cleanse the Self.
And there will be thunderbolts in the clear sky.
Tear apart the illusions and the clothing of the pupa.

Bing Shen Year Second Month of Winter
Wudang White Horse Mountain
Five Immortals Temple Xing De

Contents

List of Illustrations

Testimonials

I am extremely grateful for Hausen having found that unadorned black book, on a fateful day in the mountains of China, for here is a true treasure and key of wisdom, able to unlock the gates to the Heart of the Dao. We, as humans, need these scriptures and teachings to guide us through life and find our destiny. Therefore, it is an honorable act, and I am proud of my brothers of the Way for bringing this text to the world. Open this book, and have no regrets.

—Lindsey Wei
Author of *The Valley Spirit: A Female Story of Daoist Cultivation*
24th Generation Dragon Gate Disciple and Founder of
Wudang White Horse Internal Martial Arts Academy

After reading *Discourse on Transforming Inner Nature*, I feel like I have washed off layers of dust from the world. Just imagine what walking this path could do! This book is indeed transformative. I will put it beside my bed and read a few passages at night. I want to work its transformations during my sleep, as well as in my waking hours. The author was a sage of the twentieth century who described methods of cultivation that are accessible to everyone. The translators convey his message using simple yet profound language, like the original text. Brilliant book, beautiful translation, lovely illustrations.

—Lorraine Wilcox L.Ac.
Translator of *Categorized Essentials of Repairing the Body*

Chinese medicine has long recognized that the mind and our emotions can be either a source of disease and pain or the fountain of health and healing, but perhaps the best modern exposition of this understanding is in the teachings of Wang Fengyi. In this book, Hausen and Akers diligently translate these simple verses allowing them to speak their profound truth to modern English readers. In doing so we are transported back a century and can hear Wang speak about, in his own words, the truth of the relationship between our Hearts and our entire well-being. To do this Wang blends themes of Confucian, Buddhist and Daoist thought, with the paradigm of the Five Phases (Elements), giving us all a clear path to understanding and self transformation.

—Dr. Henry McCann

Author of *Pricking the Vessels: Bloodletting Therapy in Chinese Medicine* and co-author of *Practical Atlas of Tung's Acupuncture*

Foreword

by Daoist Renunciate Xing De (Li Shifu)

(1964–)

化性谈

是一篇很好的自我完善提升的文章。在学习和完善自我的过程中，我们的执着，我们的贪，嗔，痴，等各种欲望，对我们的身，心，灵的提升有巨大的影响和阻挡。升华和进化是宇宙万物的主题，在这个星球上我们有了肉体，就会受到阴阳五行，生老病死，诸多规律，纬度，频率等等各种限制。天地万物生生灭灭，时间，空间，生命，如梦如幻。什么才是宇宙的真理？生命的真谛？它的源头在哪里？过去我们受到父母的，朋友的，社会的等等教化。在我们的大脑中已经形成了固有的，短见的，局限的思考认知。让我们先放下来，让我们的大脑放电进入零点，不受外在事物的影响和刺激。让我们把目光收回来，向内听，向内看，向内寻找，我们就会发现一扇崭新的大门。

湖北十堰张湾武当山天马峰
白马山五仙庙兴德

Discourse on Transforming Inner Nature

Discourse on Transforming Inner Nature is a great treatise for the perfection and elevation of the "I." In the process of one's studies and the perfection of the "I," our attachments, avarice, stupors and any kind of desire exert mighty influences on and constitute barriers for the elevation of our Body, Heart and the Divine Soul.

Sublimation and evolution are the main topic and theme of the Ten Thousand Things in the universe. On this celestial planet we are endowed with our physical body, a body of flesh, which is the reason why we are subjected to all types of confinements and restrictions of Yin-Yang, the Five Elements, Birth-Aging-Sickness-Death [the four miseries of human life], and a multitude of laws, rules, dimensions, frequencies, and so on.

Heaven and Earth and the Ten Thousand Things, life after life and extinction after extinction, time, space, and Life-Destiny are as if a dream, as if an illusion:

"What are the universe's Principles of Truth then?
What are the True Essences and meanings of one's Life-Destiny?
Where are its origin and source?"

In the past we received education and instructions from our father and mother, our friends, society, and so on, through which we transformed. In our brains this has already formed innate, short-sighted and limited contemplation and recognition.

This treatise allows us to let go at first and it allows our brain's electrical impulses to enter Point Zero, not being under the influence and stimulus of external matters. It furthermore enables us to retrieve our eye's illumination, shine and radiance, enables us to listen inwards, to gaze inwards, to seek inwards, and therefore we will discover a totally new great gateway.

Hubei Shi Yan City Zhang Wan District
Mount Wudang Heavenly Horse Peak
White Horse Mountain
Five Immortals Temple Abbot Xing De

Preface

by Catherine Despeux

The text translated here, *Discourse on Transforming Inner Nature* [hua xing tan 化性談], introduces the reader into the heart of Neo-Confucian thought. The author Wang Fengyi [王凤仪 1864–1937] was a Mongol from a simple background, as his biography portrays him as a poor and illiterate peasant, a herdsman who watched over animals. He, however, was not without culture and worked to defend Confucianism. After being married at the age of twenty-three to a woman named Bai Shoukun [白守坤], with whom he would have a son, Wang Fengyi, at the age of thirty-five, would come to "realize the Way" according to Chinese terms, which means he reached some kind of self-accomplishment and found the meaning of his life and his Way.

Wang Fengyi lived at a time of great changes in China, shaken by the confrontation with Western modernism. The Manchu Qing dynasty [1644–1911] was collapsing and making place for a republic seeking to enter into modernity, while keeping its national identity being confronted with a Western model that was imposing itself. There were several scholar movements rising from multiple pockets of resistance against the foreign Manchu dynasty and the Western invaders. These movements took part in the emergence of so-called "societies of redemption," including the one to which Wang Fengyi belonged.

As a movement of defending their own culture the Universal Society of the Way and Virtue [wan guo dao de hui 萬國道德會] was formed at the beginning of the twentieth century. It was one of the best examples for a movement of spiritual transformation. It was inaugurated on the 28th of September, in 1921, on Confucius' birthday by Jiang Shoucheng [1875–1926]. He was a member of the Confucian community of Kang Youwei, and one of the most famous Confucians of the nineteenth century, who elaborated the ideal theory of "Great Harmony" [da tong 大通] and was, just before he died, the president of this universal society [1926–1927].

Wang Fengyi gave great impetus to this society that had eight million members, a quarter of the population, in the northeast of China in the years around 1930. He became an itinerant doctor and preacher of Confucian morals and, as such, was celebrated as a saintly peasant, a virtuous man, and often nicknamed "Wang the Benevolent" or "Wang the Virtuous." He contributed to a volunteer movement to develop schools for girls that in 1925 had established around two hundred and fifty schools across Manchuria. He adamantly insisted on the role of women, mothers, wives and stepdaughters to maintain social harmony and the well-being of the family.

Wang's schools emerged under the umbrella of the Universal Society of the Way and Virtue and in 1933 this society comprised five hundred branches, four hundred schools and two hundred thousand students in northeast China. Although its activities were stopped by the authorities with the advent of Mao in 1949, it continued in secret. With the policy of openness toward religions in the years around 1980, the movement re-emerged, especially in the northeast of China [Liaoning, Jilin, Heilongjiang], where its members preached filial piety and Wang Fengyi's healing methods.

Indeed, one main characteristic of Wang Fengyi's thought lies in the link he establishes between health and an individual's ethical and spiritual behavior towards oneself and towards others. Lineages of local therapists were reorganized in so-called "farms" in the northeast of China. They preached stories, held conferences and confession sessions or produced writings introducing the cosmological order of the Five Elements and how to reach this ideal harmony. This idea is not new. Since antiquity medicine scriptures have been insisting on the correspondence between the cosmological order and the order in the country, as well as in society and in the human body; however, Wang Fengyi makes associations of the cosmological order and the ethical order of Neo-Confucians in much more detail.

The doctrine and the practices elaborated by Wang Fengyi are founded on confidence in oneself, knowledge of oneself, and realization of oneself. This way, being deeply influenced by the thought of the Neo-Confucianist Wang Yangming, seeks to find the root of life and the links between Heaven, Earth and Humans from everyone's own experience. There is no hesitation to borrow concepts from the three main doctrines of Chinese thought, Buddhism, Daoism and Confucianism, and to draw parallels between similar notions of these three streams of thought.

Wang Fengyi starts off with the example of Yin and Yang in nature and the theory of the Five Elements [Wood, Fire, Earth, Metal, Water], which are simultaneously the breath of nature ruling at each season of the year. The Five Elements are predominant during each season as primordial energy of one of the Five Organs, an energy that manifests by the proper functioning of the organ and by an emotion or "movement of the soul" associated to it. Thus, in spring, the breath of Wood is dominant. In the human body the real microcosm functions like the macrocosm. The breath of Wood expresses itself in the Liver, which is associated with the normal expression of anger. To these

Five Elements, their organs and emotions Wang Fengyi would add the Five Cardinal Virtues. If the harmony of a person and of society depends on the culturalization of those qualities, the health of the individual also depends on it.

Wang Fengyi's thought is not wholly unknown to the Western public, as Sabine Wilms already translated another text of this author, the *Twelve Characters* [wang feng yi shi er zi xin zhuan 王鳳儀十二字薪傳] into English. German doctor Heiner Fruehauf considers it the ideal introduction to this powerful healing method for the Western world. In this work, Wang explains that humans have Three Natures: a Heavenly Nature [tian xing 天性], that is his/her natural disposition, a composite nature [bing xing 禀性], that is his/her propensity to impose him/herself on others, and a nature acquired by habit [bing xing 禀性]. Wang Fengyi's goal is to return to the Heavenly Nature, or Inner Nature, ordinarily obstructed by the two other types of nature.

The *Discourses,* very didactic, expose the basic notions of Wang Fengyi's thought on the Five Elements, the Five Cardinal Virtues of Confucianism, and the search of harmony between Body, Spirit and Inner Nature. They reveal, maybe more than any other of his writings, the Buddhist aspects of his thought, especially in his twelfth and last chapter, "The Transformation of Inner Nature." The emphasis is placed on letting go, on abandoning everything, as a master of Chan/Zen Buddhism said, "The place of awakening is where we abandon Body and Life." This chapter is also the continuation of the Daoist thought of Zhuang Zi who advocated "having a mind like cold ashes." It is not insignificant to notice that nowadays Wang Fengyi's belief system is also conveyed in a temple that is associated with the

Wudang Mountains, considered to be a great Daoist center. This shows that beyond the cleaving into schools this thought beneficial to the health of body and mind did continue.

The *Discourse on Transforming Inner Nature* translated by Johan Hausen, an acupuncturist passionate for Chinese culture and having spent several years studying in China, completes the *Twelve Characters* purposefully. It will be especially appreciated that this translation, very elegant and remarkably right, is bilingual, and introduces not only the English and the Chinese characters, but also their pronunciation transcribed in the phonetic system named pinyin. This work can thus be a real learning manual of the basics of Chinese thought and its key concepts. It gives a concrete testimony on the one hand of how Chinese medicine includes the different aspects of the individual within disease and on the other hand the role of the therapist who far from being content with only applying a medical technique also plays the role of psychotherapist and advises the patient on his/her life choices and behaviors. To the Westerner it sheds an interesting light on how to approach disease. Moreover it makes one ponder about the close links existing between the behavior of an individual, his/her environment and his/her disease. It invites one to take hold of one's own destiny, and to take care of one's health in simple and accessible ways.

—Catherine Despeux
June, 2017

Prologue

Introduction by the Authors

Whether happy or sad, content or angry, or if one is just plain injured, the Human Realm is often the realm of suffering, though without hardship how could anyone have an opportunity to become stronger and well tempered? In this regard, something we all have in common are the endless thoughts and emotions washing over and running through our minds and bodies, thoughts on thoughts on thoughts.

This, for some, is not so difficult, for others it is quite a challenge, yet all of us have many thoughts and feelings that are felt to excess and this leads to imbalances in the mind, body and eventually the spirit. It does not matter if it begins in the mind or if it begins in the body, the disharmonies within you could likely be balanced using the Five Elements based methods presented within this book. The process of studying or reciting theses words will naturally further one's ability to grow and learn as a human being. Put another way, the *Discourse on Transforming Inner Nature* could help one to become more aware of the ebb and flow of one's own emotions, actions and reactions, which could lead one to see oneself in honesty. This then would allow one to transform oneself (and help others transform themselves) into compassionate, giving and strong Spirits.

The body contains, carries and nourishes the mind and the mind directs the body and senses when it has needs to take care of. Many people seek wellness in their Heart, Mind and Spirit and forget that the Body is as important. Some seek wellness in

1

the body and forget how important it is to tend to their heart, mind and spirit. It is necessary to balance all of these.

Often people, knowingly or unknowingly, will give into some personal and familiar version of physical and/or emotional un-wellness and accept it as part of their life. In this way so many people batter themselves with discomfort or their emotional excesses by getting caught in their wants, desires and/or regrets with no understanding that it is essential to acknowledge one's part in un-wellness and the difficult process of self healing. And in this regard, most people will only learn to bend if they first are broken.

On a personal level, I have been living with and working to transform the disharmonies of the chronic pain condition known as fibromyalgia for about twenty years now. At times, the hardest part of dealing with fibromyalgia is not the immense and constant pain, but instead, it comes from dealing with the thought processes and feelings that come with chronic pain. Yet it is through this experience that I have come to understand the extent of my ability to influence my body, mind and spirit health, be it positively or negatively.

I have experienced how frustration and sadness, and even elation and joy can lead to emotional imbalances, physical pain, as well as organ and/ or energetic disharmonies. With fibromyalgia, if I am emotionally unbalanced, there is immediate and noticeable effect in my body. I can physically feel how and where my emotions create disharmonies. As Wang Fengyi and many others have pointed out, there is a clear connection between emotions, energy and organ function. Even if one were to approach this concept from the opposite direction of physical injury addressed into emotional disharmonies, these imbalances can be routed out with this healing method.

For me, my life experience, though constant and relentlessly difficult at times, is a blessing. I was given this life and so I am living to the best of my ability and though I do not recommend a "pain as a teacher" based method of achievement, if you happen to be living with pain in your heart, mind and/or body, you can use this difficulty to transform it into something useful and full of understanding. You can become stronger and more able, clearer in heart and mind. The potential for relief increases if one also has an accompanying Nei Dan (Internal Alchemy), Yang Sheng Gong (Long Life Skills), Qi Gong (Breath/ Energy Skills) and/or Tai Ji practice. I know this is possible as it was and is through practicing and studying these methods I have found great ability to shift my consciousness and body experience and therefore I have been able to find an inner calming and balancing of my physical strength and comfort.

As I see it, life is about being present, accepting difficulty as if it were the same as ease and showing gratitude for wellness and insight even when it comes from bitterness. As time goes on you may find that your perception of what is disharmony and wellness shifts to understand that disharmony births wellness and wellness births disharmony, therefore, adversity is to be experienced in the same light as ease. This allows life's bitterness to taste sweet.

May this translation help those who seek to transform their lives, to perhaps grow as beings and not just within this Earthly Realm. If one is receptive to the ideas and sometimes difficult reflections contained within this book there is much to be gained from its study.

—Jonas Todd Akers
May, 2017

放下来。

Put it down.

The story of the translation you hold in your hands is inseparably intertwined with my personal story. Since I consider myself first and foremost to be a translator and not an author, academic or scholar, I was strongly adverse to the idea of writing an introduction from the onset. After all, this work is not the slightest about me. Eventually I was persuaded and it helped me express and show my respect and gratitude for the transmissions of the teachings I received. Wang Fengyi's words speak for themselves, therefore I would like to seize this opportunity to explain why his doctrine struck me so dramatically, as to spending the better of two years to convey his thoughts to the Western World. I will attempt to show how the teachings that I was fortunate to receive by my master Li Shifu in China are utterly in integral synchronicity with the lore of Wang Fengyi's transmissions. These three words, "Put it down," which are embellishing the front cover with Wang Fengyi's portrait, were chosen and drawn by my master in calligraphy style to aptly summarize the content of the scripture contained herein. Without this magical place, the Five Immortals Temple, and Li Shifu's eye-opening lessons, this book would have not only never have come into fruition, but I would have never crossed paths with its riveting words. It was predestined to happen.

On a misty day in fall atop of White Horse Mountain in Hubei Province I sat down next to my master's seat in the common room, also serving as the frugal reception room for guests. A pile of books was towering in the corner of the benches.

I flicked through them, more out of boredom than the search for wisdom or the wish to find an intriguing read. Just thinking about delving into one of them was causing me a headache, let alone the ones written in classical Chinese. Being a slow reader to begin with, having to figure out and decipher classical Chinese was not an exciting task to ponder about or to look forward to at all. Suddenly a little black book caught my attention. It appeared simple, thin and unadorned. Moreover it did not bear any name or title on its front, but resembled one of those scripture books that are often handed out for free in temples and shrines to worshippers. Three black Chinese letters were written on its first page: "化性谈," *Discourse on Transforming Inner Nature.* I immediately assumed that it was Daoist in nature, since the concept of "Inner Nature" or "Inner Character" is of paramount importance within Daoist cultivation and the ultimate goal of immortality. However this concept is not limited to Daoism, as it is also interwoven into Buddhist beliefs and refinement practices. My interest was invoked strongly, to say the least.

At that point in my life I would have considered it highly unlikely for me to ever try my hands at a text and scripture steeped deeply in Confucian values and ideology. After all I had my plate more than full studying, grinding and tempering myself, as well as facilitating programs in a Daoist temple as a translator. As I started to get my teeth into it, however, I was fascinated and engulfed deeper by the drawn parallels between Buddhism, Daoism and Confucianism in a very clear, precise and to-the-point language without fanciness, without flamboyance and without ambivalence. The small black book became my daily companion. I implemented a ritual to sit down next to the Temple of the Bodhisattva of Compassion,

Guan Shi Yin Pu Sa [观世音菩萨], absorbing the last rays of sunshine in autumn and solidifying what I had learnt from my master through immersing myself into this scripture. Eventually it was through Li Shifu's encouragement and patience from which I drew the energy and perseverance to make this scripture into a published book.

Whereas Wang Fengyi's life will be discussed in more detail in a separate section, it is inevitable to shed some light on Li Shifu's background in order to explain the meaning behind his calligraphy words, "Put it down." Li Shifu is currently the abbot of the Five Immortals Temple on White Horse Mountain, one of seventy-two peaks in the Wudang mountain range. He has been a renunciate following the Great Dao for more than twenty years and is the last remaining lineage holder of several sects. During most of the year he teaches courses on Taiji, Daoist medicine, Qi Gong and Kungfu to foreigners who are willing to weather all simple living conditions in the search for knowledge and broadening of their horizons. In his classes he often expounds on the deeper meaning of the requirement to "Put it down," as the concept not only has psychological and mental implications, but also materialistic: "If you have nice food, nice clothes and live in a nice environment, you are never satisfied."

Li Shifu's master urged him to let go of even pondering about bitterness and suffering, such as carrying veggies up the mountain for lengthy times. Let even go of the bag of supplies that you shoulder on a yoke for two and a half hours during the trip.

Let go of the impetus and drive to become rich and have a high income. In order to earn a salary and wages you lose your life and the time of your life. What is more important? Is life or money more important? The expense of life-time could be compared to spending money in order to gain something else. Unfortunately your time is too short. To challenge your desires is the hardest thing. If you want a comfortable life, you ought to work very hard, which results in tiredness and a large portion of your life will be gone. Life comes in exchange for wealth. This is a common person's life.

Li Shifu would frequently warn about the difficulty of "Putting it down" and letting go of property, belongings and money. He would underpin its inherent risks by paraphrasing the famous words of Mathew [19; 24] in the bible:

我又告诉你们，骆驼穿过针的眼，
比财主进上帝的国还容易呢！

Again I tell you, it is easier for a camel
to go through the eye of a needle
than for someone who is rich
to enter the kingdom of God.

It might be surprising to Westerners that a Daoist priest refers to the bible. Li Shifu would usually tap into eclectic sources of insightful knowledge during his lectures. This can be attributed to his education making him erudite in many religious teachings, including Christianity, Catholicism, Buddhism, Daoism and Islam. He read the bible numerous times and often astonished students by drawing parallels between different religious and spiritual doctrines. At times I wondered whether he accumulated his wisdom over many lives. It was always a rather humbling experience for me as a Westerner to be lectured on the Christian bible by a Chinese Daoist. Despite not being raised as a pious Christian or having shown much devotion to the faith of the church, I have always been fascinated by the parallels and similarities between the East and the West, the Occident and the Orient. For instance the Chinese Confucian philosopher Mencius, an advocate of the doctrine of humanity and benevolence, came to an identical conclusion with Mathew:

为 富 不 仁 ， 为 仁 不 富 。

If one's aim is wealth, one cannot be benevolent;
If one's aim is benevolence, one cannot be wealthy.

Mencius was of the opinion that benevolence and gain are at conflict with each other and cannot exist harmoniously at the same time. It could be argued that any humane, philanthropic and empathetic impulse is smothered by the selfish striving and pursuit of riches. Selfishness is simply at odds with compassion, in discordance with the fellow-feeling of giving up the "Self" and contrary to the participation in the so-called collective-affective community. Furthermore the pool to draw money from is finite, and therefore accumulating riches on one end subsequently ensues in poverty on the other side. Making profits will inevitably come at the expense of others.

Since "Putting it down" is a decisive and unavoidable step as the foundation for higher cultivation endeavors in Daoism and Buddhism, Wang Fengyi's scripture could be deemed a stepping stone and springboard in the bigger perspective of cultivation objectives. Through the process of "Putting it down" you eventually arrive at the end stage, where even the shell of the physical body has to be put down. Many teachers of the past ultimately did let go of it.

In the *Forty-Nine Barriers,* a cultivation manual written by Li Shifu in one night, this barrier is called the "Barrier of Life and Death," alluding to the shedding of the physicality. High-level demons will come at you at the "Barrier of Life and Death." Observe them blandly and emotionlessly despite ghosts appearing to hit and kill you. If you get scared, it is over. It seems at first contradictory, however without this bodily form there is no vehicle and carrier to study, elevate and sublimate yourself.

Li Shifu urges listeners not to get attached to the boat. "Let go once you get to the bank on the other side. If you are attached to the body, you will be unable to go ashore. For the time being in this dimension care for and protect your 'Smelly Skin Sack,' and the Qi of the Five Zang-Organs." Chapter 40 in the *Forty-Nine Barriers* states:

> *One's body is a great gift and should be used*
> *as a boat to cross the river to enlightenment,*
> *as a ladder ascending to the Heavens.*
> *We must be determined to forge ahead perseveringly*
> *towards the purification of our spirit and towards ascension.*
> *We must make this accomplishment in this lifetime,*
> *as we cannot expect this opportunity in future lives.*

Since Wang Fengyi's core principles revolve around Confucianism, he was reverently called "the Confucian Sage" by his followers. As the scripture readily resorts to Confucian concepts, it is warranted to draw a brief outline at this point. Li Shifu and Wang Fengyi equally were both raised in environments of Confucian education, which has been deeply engrained in every part of Chinese life and society up to date. Therefore it comes to no surprise that Confucianism is one of the supporting pillars of Wang Fengyi's ideology and that both, Wang Fengyi and Li Shifu, are proponents of the "Unification of the Three Teachings" [san jiao he yi 三教合一], namely Confucianism, Buddhism and Daoism. Even politicians such as the current president of the People's Republic of China Xi Jin Ping [习近平] quoted Confucius in recent years, in a tone very reminiscent of the Christian bible:

己所不欲，勿施于人。

What you yourself do not desire,
do not impose on others.

The similarity to Mathew [7; 12] might strike readers who are well versed in the bible:

So whatever you wish that others would do to you,
do also to them, for this is the Law and the Prophets.

To my embarrassment, it took me many years before I came to the realization that the Five Immortals I was daily bowing and prostrating to were in fact honoring the Five Confucian Virtues of benevolence, righteousness, etiquette, wisdom and faith in their respective names. Amongst them the Third Immortal Grandfather [san xian ye 三仙爷], the alchemist and diviner, represents etiquette and proper conduct, or "Li" [礼] in Chinese, which is another major theme in Wang Fengyi's *Discourse on Transforming Inner Nature.*

In chapter 38 of the *Dao De Jing* Lao Zi states:

失道而后德
失德而后仁
失仁而后礼
失礼而后义。

When the Dao is lost, only Virtue is left.
When Virtue is lost, only benevolence is left.
When benevolence is lost, only etiquette is left.
When etiquette is lost, only righteousness is left.

One of the main aspects of Confucian etiquette is the establishing of rites. All religious and philosophical schools resort to the implementation of precepts, commandments, rituals and discipline. It is worth briefly analyzing the many meanings that the Chinese word for precept [jie 戒] can take on depending on its context of use. In addition to "precept," it could also be interpreted as "warning," "guarding" or "admonishment."

Therefore Christians abide by the Ten Commandments. And, equally, the three teachings of China—Confucianism, Buddhism and Daoism—all have set in stone certain rules and regulations. For instance Confucianists rely on the "Eight Pillars" as their guideline:

孝悌忠信礼仪廉耻。

Respect for one's parents, brotherhood, loyalty, faith,
propriety, chivalry, incorruptibility and humility.

Buddhists comply with their own set of precepts, such as the prohibition of alcohol, while the strictness in Daoism is unprecedented, numbering one thousand two hundred precepts at the most. Complete Reality Founding Father Wang Chong Yang adopted the "Unification of the Three Teachings" [san jiao he yi 三教合一] and therefore required all his disciples to be familiar with scriptures from all three doctrines, including the Buddhist *Heart Sutra* [xin jing 心经], the Confucian *Classic of Filial Piety* [xiao jing 孝经] and the Daoist *Classic of The Way and Virtue* [dao de jing 道德经].

The Dragon Gate Sect founded by Patriarch Qiu Chu Ji takes it a step further by upholding "The Great Precepts of the Threefold Altar" [san tan da jie 三坛大戒], which are divided into the "Initial Truths Precepts" [chu zhen jie 初真戒], the "Intermediate Bounded-Finite Precepts" [zhong ji jie 中极戒], and the "Celestial Immortals Precepts" [tian xian jie 天仙戒].

The purpose of precepts could be best explained allegorically according to Li Shifu. We commence at the stage of children. "Today I wrote unwell. Today I did an un-round drawing." But over time it becomes rounder and less jagged. Elementary school students have to sit up straight and they have to learn how to write:

横要平，竖要直。

Horizontal stroke flat, vertical stroke straight.

As if it were calligraphy, at first draw a round circle in both directions, clockwise and anti-clockwise. It is not a drawing. It is a line first, in the shape of a circle. Moreover turn the brush as if it was a compass. It is necessary for it to be perfectly round. Once children have formed these habits, you can get rid of the rules and seek the origin. Daoist renunciates, for instance, have certain clothes and hats that are worn in a certain way. Who set it like that? It could be compared to a tree as you seek starting from the branches reversing to the roots. Why are images and statues now in place in religions? Their function is to teach small children. Precepts function as a stick to hit their butts. The stick is hung on the wall. In China it is called the "Warning Ruler" [jie chi 戒尺], the teacher's bastinado. Interestingly it incorporates the Chinese word for "precept," giving clues to its original meaning and connotation. If you do not listen, you will get hit. In the same fashion the precepts of religion tell you to do things like this or like that. Thus precepts are meant to control the mind, for example "You shall not kill." You consequently make a promise, a vow or a pledge to follow those precepts. Teachers of the past, who had entered the door, i.e. had entered religious sects, would not instruct a person unless that person had taken the "Vast and Great Promise" [hong shi da yuan 宏誓大愿]. Without restrictions and restraints the teachers reckoned that you would dare to do anything. Just take the laws in society. What would society look like without laws? Especially the study of the Dao is very strict, since students' mistakes would reflect back as their teacher's failures:

学 生 不 好 , 老 师 受 牵 连 。

When the student is bad, the teacher is embroiled.

While Daoism is often associated in the West with the ubiquitous core phrase "The Dao follows the natural way" or in New Age circles interpreted as to "Go with the flow," it has been misused, exploited and served as an excuse for laziness, inertia and apathy. A myriad of actions could be defended and justified by giving it the label of so-called naturalness and spontaneity. Li Shifu adamantly underlines that it is a process from un-natural to natural. It is a big mistake and error if you normally do not have these rules set in place. In China people cross the road as it happens. It is natural for them; crossing the road whenever and wherever they want. You must accord with society's environments and society's requirements. If you only did what you like, it would be as if without precepts in a temple or without laws in society. It would be all about selfish desire coming from your molecules. If Moses had acted on the basis of his likes when leading the Israelites out of Egypt, he would have certainly dispersed them all, as the journey was hard, tiring and carried the risk of starvation.

The stern requirement of following the precepts meticulously is instilled upon you by your "Formulist" masters. Li Shifu once visited a market to buy a product for three Chinese Yuan. The saleswoman gave him seventy Chinese Yuan back instead of seven, hence he returned to clear it up. It is not a matter of the scale, size or amount. Regardless of how little it is and what it is, stealing is stealing. For your "Formulist" masters it does not matter how big the sum of money is, in fact just to think about stealing is breaking the precept. Only once you grasped these principles, could you do it naturally. The initial form or substance is superseded by the formless, and in the end from the formless springs forth something anew. Li Shifu likened it to a black hole being the beginning of new life as you can emerge in a new form.

Whereas Confucianism places utmost importance on "subduing the self and acting in accord to etiquette," Daoism considers the Confucian core value as a tool and a means to an end. The *Dao De Jing* in chapter 38 exemplifies the limitations and pitfalls of etiquette by pointing out:

夫礼者，中信之薄，而乱之首。

Now etiquette is a superficial expression of loyalty and faith;
And the beginning of disorder.

On the contrary, the objective of the Great Dao is to unify people with Heaven and Earth. When etiquette is internalized and has become second nature, there is no need for rules and rites anymore. But initially they are utterly necessary. Li Shifu employed the analogy of a river that grinds down the stones until they have no edges anymore and are perfectly round. The water of the river represents the hardships, the rules and the regulations of cultivation. It is paramount to be fully aware that you are in the water. Once you forget it, it marks the fatal end.

In his thirty years of cultivation Li Shifu has not encountered a single master or teacher promoting comfort; none of his teachers did, regardless whether Islam, Buddhism, Daoism or Christianity. He would jokingly utter that no Great Teacher came out of a five-star hotel. Muslims prostrate five times a day and that is not even hard to endure for some people. This concept has to do with the shortcomings, defects and weak points of people. To demand more of them would make it even harder for them to persevere through the precepts. There is a common saying, depicting that constant effort will bring success and enable you to accomplish any goal you have set your mind:

水滴石穿，磨杵成针。

The dripping water pierces the stone;
The steel pole is ground down into a needle.

Wang Fengyi not only adopted a philosophical system, but also applied it as a unique healing system that eventually conferred him the title "the Virtuous King" as a wordplay of his surname Wang, meaning "King." The second pillar of Wang Fengyi's healing system is the commonly known Five Elements Theory. It might seem surprising that despite Daoist and Chinese medicine hinging firmly on the Five Element system, Wang Fengyi's viewpoint is characterized by some remarkable distinctions from the standard interpretations. He further divides the Five Elements into the Five Confucian Virtues, namely benevolence or humanity [ren 仁], chivalry or righteousness [yi 义], etiquette or propriety [li 礼], wisdom [zhi 智] and faith or trust [xin 信]. Furthermore, Wang Fengyi encompasses their counterparts or vices, namely anger [nu 怒], hatred [hen 恨], resentment [yuan 怨], vexation [nao 恼], and annoyance [fan 烦].

To enter deeply into the Five Elements goes beyond the scope of this introduction and there is plenty of literature delving into this subject. The emotional aspect of the Five Elements itself serves as an intricate system that can be applied in very versatile ways, for instance as emergency remedy, utilizing the Controlling Cycle. Li Shifu recounts an incident about a man who suffered from stomach cancer, excess in the Stomach and Stomach Fire. At that time saving the patient's life was at stake and urgent help was paramount. Initially the patient was deliberately ignored by the doctor for a long time. When he eventually was attended to, the doctor accused him of being a hypochondriac, although the patient was in excruciating pain. As a consequence the patient got absolutely mad to the point of spitting out the toxins from his stomach. Immediately the doctor explained that his own unkind behavior was part of the required treatment. The patient, moreover, was prescribed herbs amongst other treatment modalities and within six months the benign tumors were cured. This is an example of the extremely difficult-to-master Controlling Cycle.

Western medicine mostly marginalizes the physical implications of emotional illness and the devastating effects of emotions. This is most probably due to the hard-to-measure immaterial and non-substantial nature of the emotional domain and research being in its infancy about the connection of body and mind. There seemed to be a noticeable shift in the medical world with the advent of psychosomatic medicine in the twentieth century, highlighting how emotional factors can contribute to a patient's physical symptoms. The prompt recognition and assessment of psychiatric problems are crucial because psychiatric comorbidity often worsens the course of medical illness, triggering significant distress in the patients and increases the costs of care such as the duration of hospital stays. There is certainly still a long road ahead, and it is quite far removed from the vantage point of Wang Fengyi's doctrine, which regards emotions as the sole root of all physical ailments.

For this reason it became a logical step for Wang Fengyi to become involved in the "Way of Virtuous People" [shan ren dao 善人道], a Confucian philosophical movement that attached importance to the resurgence of morality focusing on the smallest unit first, the familial interaction, and expanding it from there to larger communities. The charismatic sermons of Wang Fengyi played a crucial part in the later leadership and dissemination of this movement. In addition to etiquette, benevolence, and righteousness, virtue is a thick red thread running through Wang Fengyi's work. Conclusively the significance of virtue in many spiritual schools, sects and movements such as Wang Feng Yi's "Way of Virtuous People" could not be overemphasized. This notion could be epitomized by one closing citation in chapter 8 from the most foundational and fundamental classic of Daoism and the Daoist family, the *Dao De Jing:*

上善若水， 水善利万物而不争。

The highest virtue shares the nature of water.
The water's virtue is of benefit to the Ten Thousand Things.
Yet it does not contend.

—Johan Hausen
May, 2017

The Life-Destiny
of Wang Fengyi

(1864–1937)

According to his biography, *Records of Dutiful Behavior* [wang feng yi du xing lu 王凤仪笃行录], he was born into an impoverished peasant family during the chaos of war. China was war-torn by many feudal states fighting for supremacy. The situation was exacerbated by the Japanese taking advantage of the civil war and choosing this time to invade and wreaking havoc on Chinese soil. It might be worth noting that to this day the tensions have not been resolved. Each time, for example, when Japanese Prime Minister Shinzo Abe pays homage to the shrines of fallen war heroes and generals there is uproar in Chinese society and people take to the streets. The Chinese consider it a slap in the face, which is understandable taking into consideration the massacres and atrocities the Japanese army committed, just one example being the infamous genocide in Nanjing in 1937. For years later it was impossible to push a spade into the ground without striking a human skull.

It is saddening to see how deeply the scars have separated those two countries that share so much of their cultural background.

Wang Fengyi was born on November 1, 1864, in Wang Jia Yin Zi village, Chaoyang, Liaoning province, China. His parents were originally from Mongolia and he had three brothers—one older, called Wang Shutian [王树田] and two younger ones, named Wang Shusen [王树森] and Wang Shuyong [王树永]. He married at the age of twenty-three, and his wife Bai Shoukun [白守坤] gave birth to their only son, Wang Guohua [王国华].

Due to poverty Wang Fengyi did not receive any formal education during his youth. Despite his benevolence, fate seemed to have been on bad terms with Wang Fengyi. He was unfortunate to suffer from a serious illness at the age of twenty-six, which made him bedridden and forced him to remain at home. He was diagnosed with abscesses in his stomach. Over five years, it progressively worsened and he escaped death by the skin of his teeth. He saw the local doctor in his search for a cure, but was not well-off enough to pay for the whole course of herbal medicines. Therefore he could only undergo half of the treatment course and was left struggling to do even light physical labour. At age thirty-five he attained the Dao after having met a vagabond traveler and wise man named Yang Bai [杨柏], who gave an account of a simple moral tale:

Once there was a young boy who came back from school and refused to study. However, his stepmother forced him to do so. The boy was unhappy and lamented, "If my mother was still alive, she would not have treated me like this, and I wouldn't have to go through this suffering because of you!" As a result the stepmother was shocked and devastated. The old family servant stepped in and taught the boy an important lesson, "Your stepmother works hard day by day to provide for your life and pay your tuition fees since your father's death, this is why you should not say mean words like that to her." The little boy realised that he was out of place and that his emotions had gotten the better of him, and immediately said that he was sorry. His stepmother awakened to her own shortcomings, since she had let it get to her so badly in the first place, and offered an apology as well.

Although this story seems quite simplistic and straightforward, it really shook up Wang Fengyi and exerted a powerful influence on him. According to his biography *Records of Dutiful Behavior* he suddenly gained a deeper understanding:

君 子 无 德 怨 自 修 ， 小 人 有 过 怨 他 人 。

When noble people lack virtue, they blame their own cultivation,
whereas lowly people blame others for their own mistakes.

He possibly became aware of the repercussions and implications of emotions on his own health condition and this story served to open his eyes to it. He perhaps concluded that negative emotions could be eradicated and that there was no need to carry them around with him. After he completely recovered he was still judgmental of others, as he could not regard others as kind-hearted and good people. He became lofty and put himself above the contaminated and tainted world. As a result he decided to starve himself to death. On the fifth day of his attempt he had a near-death experience, as he shed the shell of his body, walking around being mindful and eventually returning to his physical body. He awoke to his gathered family members being utterly concerned about him. He grasped that death was not the answer, nor would he be able to provide for his family after his passing and, consequently, he accepted that good and bad are both part of this world and that it was his duty to look after his family.

Shortly after he let go of his judgmental attitude a local warlord seized his close friend, Yang Bai [杨柏], because he had an argument with some racketeers. The government was collaborating with the gangsters. Wang Fengyi was scared for the life of his friend and was highly agonized for several days.

Eventually he threw all caution overboard and made his way to jail, having found peace that he might have to pay the ultimate sacrifice of death. For a peasant and farmer like Wang Fengyi it posed a tremendous threat to defy the higher powers of the government authorities. It was around midnight when Wang Fengyi and his cousin closed in on the prison. All of a sudden the dark night turned as bright as if it were daytime, lasting for approximately twenty minutes. However only Wang Fengyi experienced this vision, while his cousin was unaware and oblivious to anything happening at this moment. Apparently Wang was instilled with prophetic powers foreseeing that his friend would not have to go through hardships for longer than three months. Yang Bai's [杨柏] underlying karmic reasons for receiving his punishment for three months was that he had mistreated his mother earlier in his life. It could be speculated that Wang entered into a trance, as his mind completely emptied, fearless of life and death.

Later Wang Fengyi ventured out, traveling through different provinces and making a living as a venerated and renowned spiritual healer. Throughout his life he did not charge for his healing services, reflecting his practice of the Confucianist virtue of benevolence. Wang piously followed the doctrine of Confucianism, which emphasizes that a person should maintain benevolence not only outside of the family, but also within the family in order to foster and nurture good relationships amongst family members. In Confucianism, the virtue of "Filial Piety" or "Respect for one's Parents" [xiao 孝] is given greatest attention in family interactions. This is the reason why up to four generations used to live under one roof assisting the upbringing of the next generations.

After his father's death Wang Fengyi committed himself to stay at his father's graveside for three years. During that time he convinced his wife to enroll at the local school, as she was uneducated and illiterate. She was aged thirty-eight at that time and succeeded to take up the profession of a school teacher eventually. Education for children was not affordable for the majority of Chinese families, as it was considered a luxury, let alone education for someone at such an advanced age and coming from a poor background. Wang Fengyi's son followed in his mother's footsteps and they both managed to become financially independent from Wang Fengyi. This in turn allowed Wang to embark on his travels, as he had fulfilled his family duties. Therefore one of his most remarkable accomplishments was the founding of countless schools ensuring the education of women, which was something rather unusual and a frowned upon undertaking at that time. He was involved in the setting up of around seven hundred schools for girls, a timeless and groundbreaking feat.

During his travel, he made speeches, told stories and helped numerous people to be healed from sickness. Wang Fengyi ascended at the age of seventy-four. When his coffin was returned to his hometown, he was received by large crowds of adherents paying homage to his last journey. On that day Wang Fengyi literally united the people from all walks of life and social strata like he had done during his lifetime in this world.

To date very few of Wang Feng Yi's teaching have been made available to the English-speaking world.

A select group in the United States has published two books on Wang Fengyi's Emotional Healing System, namely *Twelve Characters: Transmission of Wang Fengyi's teachings* by Sabine Wilms and *Let the Radiant Yang Shine Forth: Lectures on Virtue* translated by Liu Zuozhi and Sabine Wilms.

Furthermore, Heiner Fruehauf published an online article titled *All Disease Comes From the Heart: The Pivotal Role of the Emotions in Classical Chinese Medicine.*

Last but not least there is Greg Golden's Shanren Dao thesis, *Cultivating Virtue as Medicine: Spiritual and Ethical Prescriptions for the Emotional Roots of Disease.*

However, Wang Fengyi's magnum opus, *The Record of the Words and Deeds of Wang Fengyi* [wang feng yi yan xing lu 王凤仪言行录], remains inaccessible to the English-speaking Western world at the time of writing this book.

Discourse on Transforming Inner Nature

化

性

谈

Hua Xing Tan

（一）

Chapter 1

不 怨 人

Bu Yuan Ren

Do Not
Resent People

我 常 研 究 ，

wo chang yan jiu,

I constantly research,

怨 人 是 苦 海 。

yuan ren shi ku hai.

resenting people is the Sea of Bitterness.

越 怨 人 ，

yue yuan ren,

The more you resent people,

心 里 越 难 过 ，

xin li yue nan guo,

the more unwell you will feel in your Heart.

以 致 不 是 生 病 ，

yi zhi bu shi sheng bing,

If the result is not disease,

就 是 招 祸 ，

jiu shi zhao huo,

then it is beckoning misfortune.

不 是 苦 海 是 什 么 ？

bu shi ku hai shi shen me?

If this is not the Sea of Bitterness, what is it then?

管 人 是 地 狱 ，
guan ren shi di yu,
Controlling people is Hell.[1]

管 一 分 ，
guan yi fen,
Controlling one part,

别 人 恨 一 分 。
bie ren hen yi fen.
others will begrudge one part.

管 十 分 ，
guan shi fen,
Controlling ten parts,

别 人 恨 十 分 。
bie ren hen shi fen.
others will begrudge ten parts.

不 是 地 狱 是 什 么 ？
bu shi di yu shi shen me?
If this is not Hell, what is then?

必 须 反 过 来 ，
bi xu fan guo lai,
One must reverse this.

能 领 人 的 才 能 了 人 间 债，

neng ling ren de cai neng liao ren jian zhai,

If one is able to guide people, one then
can settle the debts between humans.

尽 了 做 人 的 道 。

jin liao zuo ren de dao.

Do your utmost to grasp the Dao
of an upright person.

能 度 人 的 就 是 神，

neng du ren de jiu shi shen,

The ones capable of delivering people
are precisely spiritual beings.

能 成 人 的 就 是 佛 。

neng cheng ren de jiu shi fo.

The ones capable of accomplishing this
perfect person, are precisely Buddhas.

君 子 求 己，

jun zi qiu ji,

The noble person seeks himself.

小 人 求 人 。

xiao ren qiu ren.

The lowly person seeks people.

君 子 无 德 怨 自 修 ，
jun zi wu de yuan zi xiu,
The noble person without virtue resents
his own cultivation.

小 人 有 过 怨 他 人 。
xiao ren you guo yuan ta ren.
A lowly person, having faults, resents other people,

嘴 里 不 怨 ，
zui li bu yuan,
outwards, speaking without resentment,

心 里 怨 ，
xin li yuan,
inwards, cherishing resentment in one's Heart.

越 怨 心 里 越 难 过 。
yue yuan xin li yue nan guo.
The more resentment, the more one is
unwell in one's Heart.

怨 气 有 毒 ，
yuan qi you du,
Resentful Qi is poisonous.

存 在 心 里 ，
cun zai xin li,
Contained in one's Heart,

不 但 难 受 ,

bu dan nan shou,

it is not only hard to endure,

还 会 生 病 ,

hai hui sheng bing,

it will also lead to disease,

等 于 是 自 己 服 毒 药 。

deng yu shi zi ji fu du yao.

as it equals eating poison yourself.

人 若 能 反 省 ,

ren ruo neng fan xing,

If people are able to be introspective,

找 着 自 己 的 不 是 (错 误) ,

zhao zhe zi ji de bu shi (cuo wu),

searching for one's own faults (mistakes),

自 然 不 往 外 怨 。

zi ran bu wang wai yuan.

naturally one will not resent outwardly.

你 能 ,

ni neng,

You will be able to

不 怨 不 能 的 ;
bu yuan bu neng de;
not resent what you are unable to do.

你 会 ,
ni hui,
You will be capable

不 怨 不 会 的 ,
bu yuan bu hui de,
of not resenting what you are incapable of

明 白 对 面 的 人 的 道 ,
ming bai dui mian de ren de dao,
and understand the Dao of the person
in front of you,

就 不 怨 人 了 。
jiu bu yuan ren le.
therefore, not resenting people.

现 今 的 人 ,
xian jin de ren,
People of today,

都 因 为 别 人 看 不 起 自 己 ,
dou yin wei bie ren kan bu qi zi ji,
because others look down on them,

就 不 乐 。

jiu bu le.

are therefore unhappy.

其 实 我 这 个 人 ，

qi shi wo zhe ge ren,

Actually I am this person:

好 就 是 好 ，

hao jiu shi hao,

Good is just good,

歹 就 是 歹 ，

dai jiu shi dai,

crooked is just crooked.

管 别 人 看 得 起 看 不 起 呢 ？

guan bie ren kan de qi kan bu qi ne?

When controlling other people,
are you thinking highly or lowly of them?

只 是 一 个 不 怨 人 ，

zhi shi yi ge bu yuan ren,

Only a person free from resentment

就 能 成 佛 。

jiu neng cheng fo.

is able to become a Buddha.

现 在 的 精 明 人 ，

xian zai de jing ming ren,

The shrewd people of today

都 好 算 账 。

dou hao suan zhang.

are all fond of reckoning accounts.

算 起 来 ，

suan qi lai,

After reckoning,

不 是 后 悔 ，

bu shi hou hui,

they either feel regret

就 是 抱 屈 ，

jiu shi bao qu,

or they feel wronged.

那 能 不 病 呢 ？

na neng bu bing ne?

Can this not create disease?

不 怨 人 三 个 字 ，

bu yuan ren san ge zi,

The three words, Without Resenting People,

妙 到 极 点 啦 ！

miao dao ji dian la!

mystery reaches its utmost!

（ 不 怨 人 是 真 阳 土 。）

(bu yuan ren shi zhen yang tu.)

(Not resenting people is the True Yang Earth.)

Outcropped pine tree

Chapter 2

不生气
不上火

Bu Sheng Qi
Bu Shang Huo

Do Not Raise Qi
Do Not Flare Up Fire[2]

43

我 常 研 究 ，

wo chang yan jiu,

I constantly research.

火 逆 的 多 吐 血 ，

huo ni de duo tu xue,

When Fire counter-flows, there will truly be
a lot of vomiting of blood.

气 逆 的 多 吐 食 。

qi ni de duo tu shi.

When Qi counter-flows, there will truly be
a lot of vomiting of food.

要 能 行 道 、

yao neng xing dao,

If you are able to walk with the Dao,

明 道 ，

ming dao,

and grasp the Dao,

气 火 就 都 消 了 。

qi huo jiu dou xiao le.

then both Qi and Fire will be extinguished.

上 火 是 『 龙 吟 』，

shang huo shi "long yin,"

Flaring-up Fire is "the Dragon Howling."

生 气 是 『 虎 啸 』，
sheng qi shi "hu xiao,"
Giving rise to Qi is "the Tiger Roaring."

人 能 降 伏 住 气 火，
ren neng xiang fu zhu qi huo,
When people are able to subdue and tame Qi and Fire,

才 能 成 道 。
cai neng cheng dao.
then they can achieve the Dao.

有 人 惹 逆 ，
you ren re ni,
If people provoke your counter-flow,

你 别 生 气 ，
ni bie sheng qi,
do not give rise to Qi.

若 是 生 气 ，
ruo shi sheng Qi,
If you give rise to Qi,

气 往 下 行 变 成 寒 。
qi wang xia xing bian cheng han.
it will descend and turn into coldness.

有事逼你，

you shi bi ni,

When a matter coerces you,

你别着急，

ni bie zhao ji,

do not get anxious.

若是着急，

ruo shi zhao ji,

If you get anxious,

火往上行变为热，

huo wang shang xing bian wei re,

Fire will travel upwards and turn into heat.

修行人，

xiu xing ren,

People who cultivate

遇好事不喜，

yu hao shi bu xi,

are not joyous encountering good events

遇坏事不愁，

yu huai shi bu chou,

and not worried encountering bad events,

气 火 自 然 不 生 ，

qi huo zi ran bu sheng,

therefore, Qi and Fire naturally
do not come into existence.

就 是 『 降 龙 伏 虎 』。

jiu shi "xiang long fu hu."

This is meant by "Subduing the Dragon
and Taming the Tiger."[3]

能 降 伏 住 ，

neng xiang fu zhu,

Being capable of "Subduing and Taming"

它 就 为 我 用 。

ta jiu wei wo yong.

can be of use to me.

降 伏 不 住 ，

xiang fu bu zhu,

Being incapable of "Subduing and Taming"

它 就 是 妖 孽 了 。

ta jiu shi yao nie le.

then becomes calamitous.

禀 性 。

bing xing.

Natural Dispositions

（怒、恨、怨、脑、烦、又称气禀性。）

(nu, hen, yuan, nao, fan, you cheng qi bing xing.)

(wrath, hatred, resentment, annoyance, and vexation,
also known as, "Qi Dispositions").

用事，

yong shi,

When they are in power,

鬼来当家，

gui lai dang jia,

ghosts will appear to manage your household affairs.

因为生气、

yin wei sheng qi,

Because of giving rise to Qi,

上火一定害病，

shang huo yi ding hai bing,

Flaring-up Fire will certainly contract illness.

生病就是被鬼给打倒了！

sheng bing jiu shi bei gui gei da dao le!

Falling sick is exactly being knocked down by ghosts!

正念一生，

zheng nian yi sheng,

As soon as upright thoughts are generated,

神 就 来 ;
shen jiu lai;
Spirits will appear at once.

邪 念 一 起 ,
xie nian yi qi,
As soon as evil thoughts arise,

鬼 就 到 。
gui jiu dao.
ghosts will appear at once.

可 惜 人 都 不 肯 当 神 ,
ke xi ren dou bu ken dang shen,
It is pitiful that all people are unwilling to act as Spirits,

甘 愿 做 鬼 !
gan yuan zuo gui!
yet, they are willing to act as ghosts!

火 是 由 心 里 生 的 ,
huo shi you xin li sheng de,
Fire is born from within the Heart.

人 心 一 动 就 生 火 。
ren xin yi dong jiu sheng huo.
Once the Human Heart stirs, it gives birth to Fire.

一 着 急 ，

yi zhao ji,

Once being anxious,

火 往 上 升 。

huo wang shang sheng.

Fire flares upwards.

一 动 念 ，

yi dong nian,

Once thoughts are stirring,

火 向 外 散 。

huo xiang wai san.

Fire is dispersed outwards.

若 能 定 住 心 ，

ruo neng ding zhu xin,

If one is able to settle the Heart,

火 自 然 下 降 。

huo zi ran xia jiang.

Fire naturally descends.

不 守 本 分 的 人 ，

bu shou ben fen de ren,

People who do not safeguard their bounds[4]

额 外 的 贪 求 ，

e wai de tan qiu,

and are demanding excesses,

火 就 妄 动 。

huo jiu wang dong.

their Fire will move frenetically.

若 能 把 心 放 下 ，

ruo neng ba xin fang xia,

If one is able to let go of one's Heart

不 替 人 着 急 ，

bu ti ren zhao ji,

and does not replace it with any human anxieties,

就 不 起 火 ，

jiu bu qi huo,

therefore not giving rise to Fire,

该 有 多 么 轻 快 ！

gai you duo me qing kuai!

one certainly will be extremely unburdened!

动 性 （ 耍 脾 气 ） 是 火 ，

dong xing (shua pi qi) shi huo,

Stirring Dispositions (having fits of temper) is Fire.

心 里 生 气 ，

xin li sheng qi,

In the Heart, if giving rise to Qi,[5]

才 是 气 。

cai shi qi.

it is only Qi.

佛 说 （七 处 心 灯），

fo shuo "qi chu xin deng,"

Buddha says "The Seven Places are the
Heart's Lantern,"[6]

我 说 不 如 陷 死 一 头 。

wo shuo bu ru xian si yi tou.

I say that it is not as good
as sinking into death headfirst.

人 心 一 死 ，

ren xin yi si.

Once the Human Heart dies,

道 心 自 生 。

dao xin zi sheng.

the Dao Heart is born by itself.

人 心 一 动 ，

ren xin yi dong

Once the Human Heart stirs,

道 心 自 灭 。

dao xin zi mie.

the Dao Heart extinguishes by itself.

争 贪 的 念 头 ,

zheng tan de nian tou,

Having thoughts of strife and greed

就 生 出 来 了 。

jiu sheng chu lai le.

is the same as life leaking out.

因 争 生 气 ,

yin zheng sheng qi,

Because strife gives rise to Qi

因 贪 上 火 ,

yin tan shang huo,

and because greed flares up Fire,

气 火 攻 心 ,

qi huo gong xin,

this Qi and Fire attack the Heart.

整 天 烦 恼 ,

zheng tian fan nao,

All day, being annoyed and vexed,

就 是 富 贵 ，

jiu shi fu gui,

this is the same as having wealth and rank,

也 没 乐 趣 ，

ye mei le qu,

as both are without joy.

所 以 古 人 治 心 ，

suo yi gu ren zhi xin,

Therefore the people of the past healed the Heart,

如 同 治 病 。

ru tong zhi bing.

similar to healing disease.

我 说 把 心 陷 死 ，

wo shuo ba xin xian si,

I say let the Heart sink into death,

多 么 省 事 ！

duo me sheng shi!

it saves a lot of troubles!

Tame tiger

我 好 处
认 不 是

Wo Hao Chu
Ren Bu Shi

My Positives &
Admitting Faults

修好的人多，

xiu hao de ren duo,

There are many people cultivating goodness,

得好的人少，

de hao de ren shao,

but there are only few achieving goodness.

是因为什么呢？

shi yin wei shen me ne?

Why is that?

就因为心里存的，

jiu yin wei xin li cun de,

It is because they keep in their Hearts

都是别人的不好，

dou shi bie ren de bu hao,

that everything is other people's evilness,

又怎能得好呢？

you zen neng de hao ne?

so how could they achieve goodness then?

找人好处是『聚灵』，

zhao ren hao chu shi "ju ling,"

Seeking people's positives is "Accumulating Divinity."

看人毛病（缺点）是『收赃』。
kan ren mao bing (que dian) shi "shou zang."
Seeking other people's faults (flaws)
is "Collecting Spoils."

『聚灵』是收阳光，
"ju ling" shi shou yang guang,
"Accumulating Divinity" is to retrieve
the Brightness of Yang.

心里温暖，
xin li wen nuan,
When it is warm inside the Heart,

能够养心；
neng gou yang xin;
one is able to nourish the Heart.

『收赃』是存阴气，
"shou zang" shi cun yin qi,
"Collecting Spoils" is to store Yin-Qi.[7]

心里阴沉，
xin li yin chen,
When there is Yin-Heaviness inside the Heart,

就会伤身。
jiu hui shang shen.
one will injure the Body.

61

人人都有好处,

ren ren dou you hao chu,

All people have positives,

就是恶人,

jiu shi e ren,

even evil people.

也有好处,

ye you hao chu,

They also have positives.

正面找不着,

zheng mian zhao bu zhu,

If they cannot be found upfront,

从反面上找。

cong fan mian shang zhao.

search for them from the backside.

所以我说,

suo yi wo shuo,

Therefore, I say

找好处是『暖心丸』,

zhao hao chu shi "nuan xin wan,"

seeking positives is "The Warming Heart Pill"

到 处 有 缘 ,

dao chu you yuan,

as there will be ties with destiny everywhere,

永 无 苦 恼 。

yong wu ku nao.

forever being without bitterness and vexation.

找 好 处 是 真 金 ,

zhao hao chu shi zhen jin,

Seeking positives is True Gold.

要 想 找 好 处 ,

yao xiang zhao hao chu,

If one wishes to seek positives,

就 得 以 志 为 根 ,

jiu de yi zhi wei gen,

then one obtains determination as one's root.

在 没 有 丝 豪 的 好 处 里 ,

zai mei you si mao de hao chu li,

Within not even a silken thread of positives,

找 出 真 好 处 来 ,

zhao chu zhen hao chu lai,

through searching, true positives
can make an appearance.

在 忍 无 可 忍 时 ，
zai ren wu ke ren shi,
When one endures more than is bearable

还 能 忍 得 住 ，
hai neng ren de zhu,
and still is capable of enduring it,

就 是 『 大 义 参 天 』。
jiu shi "da yi can tian."
that is precisely "The Great Righteousness
Reaching to the Skies."

认 不 是 生 智 慧 水 ，
ren bu shi sheng zhi hui shui,
Admitting faults gives birth
to the Waters of Wisdom.

水 能 调 五 味 ，
shui neng tiao wu wei,
Water is able to regulate the Five Tastes,

合 五 色 ，
he wu se,
unify the Five Colors,

随 方 就 圆 。
sui fang jiu yuan.
and adapt itself to all circumstances.

人 的 性 子 ,

ren de xing zi,

People's Inner Nature,

要 能 炼 得 像 水 一 样 ,

yao neng lian de xiang shui yi yang,

if it can be refined to appear as Water,

就 成 道 了 。

jiu cheng dao le.

it then will precisely become the Dao.

所 以 古 人 说 『 上 善 如 水 』。

suo yi gu ren shuo "shang shan ru shui."

Therefore, the ancient people said,

"The highest virtue is like water."

人 和 天 地 是 一 体 ,

ren he tian di shi yi ti,

Humans share one body with Heaven and Earth.

天 下 的 事 都 是 自 己 分 内 的 事 ,

tian xia de shi dou shi zi ji fen nei de shi,

and all affairs under Heaven are matters

of one's own Duty.

世 界 没 好 ,

shi jie mei hao,

If the world is not well,

咱 们 那 能 没 有 不 是 ？

zan men na neng mei you bu shi?

how could we be without fault?

不 是 （ 错 误 ） 到 处 都 有 ，

bu shi (cuo wu) dao chu dou you,

Faults (mistakes) exist everywhere,

低 头 也 是 、

di tou ye shi,

no matter if you lower your head,

抬 头 也 是 、

tai tou ye shi,

no matter if you lift your head,

睁 眼 也 是 、

zheng yan ye shi,

when you open your eyes,

闭 眼 也 是 。

bi yan ye shi.

or when you close your eyes.

看 妻 子 不 好 是 低 头 不 是 ，

kan qi zi bu hao shi di tou bu shi,

Perceiving one's wife as bad
is the fault of lowering the head.

看 老 人 不 对 是 抬 头 不 是 ,
kan lao ren bu dui shi tai tou bu shi,
Perceiving one's elders as incorrect
is the fault of lifting one's head.

看 别 人 不 对 是 睁 眼 不 是 ,
kan bie ren bu dui shi zheng yan bu shi,
Perceiving other people as wrong
is the fault of opening one's eyes.

心 里 寻 思 别 人 不 对 是 闭 眼 不 是 。
xin li xun si bie ren bu dui shi bi yan bu shi.
Pondering in one's Heart about other people's
wrongs is the fault of closing your eyes.

依 我 说 ,
yi wo shuo,
According to what I say,

有 不 明 白 的 道 、
you bu ming bai de dao,
if there are incomprehensible ways

不 会 做 的 事 ,
bu hui zuo de shi,
and things one is incapable of doing,

都 是 不 是 ，

dou shi bu shi,

it is everything else's fault.

人 要 能 找 着 本 分 ，

ren yao neng zhao zhe ben fen,

When people want to be able to find
contentment with their Duty,

才 知 道 不 是 。

cai zhi dao bu shi.

only then will they be aware of faults.

人 把 天 理 丢 了 、

ren ba tian li diu le,

Only after people lose the Principles of Heaven,

道 理 迷 了 、

dao li mi le,

confuse the Principles of the Dao,

情 理 亏 了 ，

qing li kui le,

and lack the Principles of Reason,

才 知 道 认 不 是

cai zhi dao ren bu shi

then will they be aware of admitting their faults

（承认不对即认错）。
(cheng ren bu dui ji ren cuo).
(admitting one's wrongs means
admitting one's mistakes).

要能把不是认真了，
yao neng ba bu shi ren zhen le,
If one is able to take one's faults seriously,

自然神清气爽、
zi ran shen qing qi shuang,
then naturally Spirit is pure, Qi is bright,

心平气和。
xin ping qi he.
the Heart is calm, and Qi is balanced.

认不是生智慧水，
ren bu shi sheng zhi hui shui,
Admitting faults gives birth to the Waters of Wisdom.

找好处生响亮金。
zhao hao chu sheng xiang liang jin.
Seeking positives gives rise to
Resonant and Shining Gold.

找好处开了天堂路，
zhao hao chu kai le tian tang lu,
Seeking positives opens the road to the Heavenly Hall.

认 不 是 闭 上 地 狱 门 。

ren bu shi bi shang di yu men.

Admitting one's faults shuts the Gate to Hell.

认 不 是 胜 服 『 清 凉 散 』，

ren bu shi sheng fu "qing liang san,"

Admitting one's faults surpasses the ingestion
of "The Clearing Cooling Powder."

找 好 处 胜 用 『 暖 心 丸 』。

zhao hao chu sheng yong "nuan xin wan."

Seeking positives surpasses the use of
"The Warming Heart Pill."

The flow of water

五行性

Wu Xing Xing

The Nature of the Five Elements[8]

我 所 以 讲 的 五 行 ，
wo suo yi jiang de wu xing,
I will now discuss the Five Elements:

是 以 木 、
shi yi mu,
Wood,

火 、
huo,
Fire,

土 、
tu,
Earth,

金 、
jin,
Metal,

水 五 个 字 代 表 来 说 的 。
shui wu ge zi dai biao lai shuo de.
and Water, and what those five words
represent as teachings.

和 佛 家 的 五 戒 、
he fo jia de wu jie,
Identical to the Buddhist Five Precepts,

道家的五元、
dao jia de wu yuan,
the Daoist Five Primordials

儒家的五常是一样的。
ru jia de wu chang shi yi yang de.
and the Confucianist Five Constants,
they are all the same.

人的苦都在性子中呢！
ren de ku dou zai xing zi zhong ne!
People's bitterness is all within Inner Nature!

不服人是阴木，
bu fu ren shi yin mu,
Not being of service to people is Yin-Wood.

好争理是阴火，
hao zheng li shi yin huo,
Being fond of arguing reason is Yin-Fire.

好怨人是阴土，
hao yuan ren shi yin tu,
Being fond of resentment is Yin-Earth.

好分辨是阴金，
hao fen bian shi yin jin,
Being fond of discrimination is Yin-Metal.

好 烦 人 是 阴 水 。

hao fan ren shi yin shui.

being fond of vexation is Yin-Water.

木 性 人 招 难 ,

mu xing ren zhao nan,

Wood-Natured people beckon difficulty.

火 性 人 受 苦 ,

huo xing ren shou ku,

Fire-Natured people suffer from bitterness.

土 性 人 受 累 ,

tu xing ren shou lei,

Earth-Natured people suffer from tiredness.

金 性 人 受 贫 ,

jin xing ren shou fen,

Metal-Natured people suffer from poverty.

水 性 人 受 气 ,

shui xing ren shou qi,

Water-Natured people suffer from bullying.[9]

像 聚 宝 盆 似 的 ,

xiang ju bao pen si de,

Be as if a vessel holding precious treasures.

内 里 有 什 么 ，

nei li you shen me,

What is inside,

就 聚 什 么 。

jiu ju shen me.

is what has been accumulated.

太 上 说 ：『 祸 福 无 门 ，

tai shang shuo: "huo fu wu men,

Tai Shang[10] said: "Fortune and misfortune are without gates,

惟 人 自 招 。』

wei ren zi zhao."

only people alone beckon them."[11]

一 点 也 不 错 。

yi dian ye bu cuo.

It is never wrong, not even a little bit.

所 以 我 说 ，

suo yi wo shuo,

Therefore I say,

好 事 歹 事 都 是 性 子 招 的 。

hao shi dai shi dou shi xing zi zhao de.

good events and bad events are all beckoned by one's Nature.

常 人 的 性 子 都 有 所 偏 。

chang ren de xing zi dou you suo pian.

Common people's Inner Nature
always deviates to some extent.

偏 于 火 的 争 理 ，

pian yu huo de zheng li,

People deviating towards Fire
are arguing reason.

偏 于 土 的 欺 人 ，

pian yu tu de qi ren,

People deviating towards Earth
are bullying others.

偏 于 金 的 伤 人 ，

pian yu jin de shang ren,

People deviating towards Metal
are harming others.

偏 于 水 的 厌 人 ，

pian yu shui de yan ren,

People deviating towards Water
are loathing others.

偏 于 木 的 顶 撞 人 。

pian yu mu de ding zhuang ren.

People deviating towards Wood
are contradicting others.

能 化 除 这 一 偏 之 性 ，
neng hua chu zhe yi pian zhi xing,
If one can transform and remove
this deviated Inner Nature,

自 然 得 道 。
zi ran de dao.
the Dao will naturally be attained.

阴 木 性 人 ，
yin mu xing ren,
Yin-Wood Natured people

抗 上 、
kang shang
contradict their superiors,

不 服 人 ，
bu fu ren,
are not of service to people,

好 生 怨 怒 气 。
hao sheng nu qi.
and are fond of generating hateful Qi.

怒 气 伤 肝 ，
nu qi shang gan,
Hateful Qi injures the liver,

头 迷 眼 花、

tou mi yan hua,

and causes muddle-headedness
and blurred vision,

两 臂 麻 木、

liang bei ma mu,

In both arms, tingling and numbness,

胸 膈 不 舒、

xiong ge bu shu,

discomfort in the chest and diaphragm,

耳 鸣 牙 痛、

er ming ya tong,

ear ringing and toothache,

瘫 痪 中 风。

tan huan zhong feng.

and paralysis and wind-stroke.

阴 火 性 人,

yin huo xing ren,

Yin-Fire Natured people are

急 躁、

ji zao,

irritable,

争理、

zheng li,

argue reason,

喜虚荣、

xi xu rong,

fond of vanity,[12]

爱面子、

ai mian zi,

concerned with saving face,

好恨人。

hao hen ren.

and fond of hating people.

恨人伤心,

hen ren shang xin,

Hating others harms the Heart

心热心跳、

xin re xin tiao,

causing Heart-Heat and palpitations,

失眠颠狂、

shi min dian kuang,

sleeplessness and madness,

音哑疔疮。

yin ya ding chuang.

and loss of voice and boils.

阴土性人，

yin tu xing ren,

Yin-Earth Natured people are

蠢笨蛮横，

chun ben man heng,

stupid, rude,

疑心重、

yi xin zhong,

suspicious

好怨人。

hao yuan ren.

and fond of resenting people.

怨人伤脾，

yuan ren shang pi,

Resenting others injures the Spleen

膨闷胀饱、

peng men zhang bao,

causing swelling, tightness,
distention, fullness

腹 痛 吐 泻、
fu tong tu xie,
abdominal pain, vomiting, diarrhea,

虚 弱 气 短 。
xu ruo qi duan.
weakness, feebleness and shortness of breath.

阴 金 性 人，
yin jin xing ren,
Yin-Metal Natured people are

残 忍 嫉 妒 （爱 小）、
can ren ji du (ai xiao),
ruthless, envious (pursuing petty gains),

虚 伪 好 辩，
xu wei hao bian,
hypocritical, fond of discriminating,

好 恼 人 。
hao nao ren.
and fond of vexing people.

恼 人 伤 肺，
fan ren shang fei,
Vexing others injures the Lungs

气喘咳嗽，

qi chuan ke sou,

causing wheezing, coughing,

肺痨咯血。

fei lao ka xue.

lung consumption, and spitting of blood.

阴水性人，

yin shui xing ren,

Yin-Water Natured people are

愚鲁迟钝、

yu lu chi dun,

simple-minded, blunt,

多忧多虑，

duo you duo lü,

worried, pensive,

好烦人。

hao fan ren.

and fond of annoying people.

烦人伤肾，

fan ren shang shen,

Annoying others injures the Kidneys

腰 腿 病 痛 ，
yao tui bing tong,
causing waist and leg ailments and pain,

遗 精 阴 痿 。
yi jing yin wei.
involuntary seminal emissions and impotence.

所 以 说 什 么 性 ，
suo yi shuo shen me xing,
Therefore, depending on the Inner Nature,

就 得 什 么 病 。
jiu de shen me bing.
one is afflicted by certain illnesses.

我 所 说 的 五 行 ，
wo suo shuo de wu xing,
What I say about the Five Elements,

和 佛 家 的 五 戒 是 一 样 的 。
he fo jia de wu jie shi yi yang de.
is the same as the Buddhist Five Precepts.

生 怒 气 （木 ）便 是 杀 ；
sheng nu qi (mu) bian shi sha;
Giving rise to hateful Qi (Wood) is murderous.

好 穿 衣 服、

hao chuan yi fu,

Being fond of nice clothes

求 好 看 （火）便 是 淫；

qiu hao kan (huo) bian shi yin;

and seeking beauty (Fire) is lewdness.

买 东 西 小 给 一 文 钱 （金）也 是 盗；

mai dong xi shao gei yi wen qian (jin) ye shi dao;

Buying items and giving a single cent less (Metal)
is also stealing.

好 吃 好 东 西 （水）便 是 酒；

hao chi hao dong xi (shui) bian shi jiu;

Being fond of eating delicious foods (Water)
is also drunkenness.

说 半 句 谎 话 （土）也 是 妄。

shuo ban ju huang hua (tu) ye shi wang.

Telling half a sentence of a falsehood (Earth)
is also lying.

真 木 是 佛 的 跟 （木 性 仁 慈），

zhen mu shi fo de gen (mu xing ren ci),

True Wood is the root of Buddha (Wood-Nature:
benevolence and compassion).

真（阳）木性人有主意、

zhen (yang) mu xing ren you zhu yi,

True (Yang) Wood-Natured people
are decisive.

能 忍 辱 ,

neng ren ru,

They are able to endure humiliation,

能 立 万 物 。

neng li wan wu.

and have the ability to found
the Ten Thousand Things.

真 火 是 神 的 跟 ,

zhen huo shi shen de gen,

True Fire is the root of the Spirit.

火 主 明 理 、

huo zhu ming li,

Fire governs the grasping of Principles,

知 时 达 务 ,

zhi shi da wu,

and knowing the time for attaining one's Duty.

能 化 万 物 ,

neng hua wan wu,

One is then able to transform
the Ten Thousand Things,

不 为 万 物 所 拘 。

bu wei wan wu suo ju.

not being restrained by the Ten Thousand Things.

真 土 是 道 的 跟 ,

zhen tu shi dao de gen,

True Earth is the root of the Dao.

信 因 果 、

xin yin guo,

Believing in Cause and Effect,[13]

能 容 能 化 ,

neng rong neng hua,

one is able to melt, one is able to dissolve,

能 生 万 物 。

neng sheng wan wu.

and one is able to give birth
to the Ten Thousand Things.

别 人 坏 是 别 人 的 因 果 ,

bie ren huai shi bie ren de yin guo,

Other people's badness is other people's
Cause and Effect.

你 不 要 怨 他 ,

ni bu yao yuan ta,

Do not resent others.

也 不 要 替 他 着 急 。

ye bu yao ti ta zhao ji.

Also, do not be anxious in their stead.

真 金 是 仙 的 根 ,

zhen jin shi xian de gen,

True Metal is the root of Immortals,

能 找 人 好 处 ,

neng zhao ren hao chu,

and it is the ability to seek people's positives.

找 好 处 生 响 亮 金 ,

zhao ren hao chu sheng xiang liang jin,

Seeking people's positives will give birth
to Resonant and Shining Gold.

和 人 聚 万 缘 ,

he ren ju wan yuan,

and accumulate Ten Thousand Destinies
with people.

有 义 气 ,

you yi qi,

Being endowed with a spirit of justice,[14]

有 果 断 力 ,

you guo duan li,

you have the power to sever from consequences.

遇事迎刃而解，

yu shi ying ren er jie,

Coming across issues, they will split
as they meet the knife's edge

能创万物。

neng chuang wan wu.

and one is able to initiate the Ten Thousand Things.

真水是圣的根，

zhen shui shi sheng de gen,

True Water is the root of Sages,

能认不是，

neng ren bu shi,

and it is the ability to admit one's faults.

认不是生智慧水。

ren bu shi sheng zhi hui shui.

Admitting one's faults gives birth
to the Waters of Wisdom.

水性柔和，

shui xing rou he,

Water's nature is gentle and soft,

能养万物。

neng yang wan wu.

it is capable of nourishing
the Ten Thousand Things.

人 如 果 得 不 着 真 五 行 ，
ren ru guo de bu zhao zhen wu xing,
If one is unable to obtain the true Five Elements,

固 执 禀 性 用 事 ，
gu zhi bing xing yong shi,
one clings to one's Natural Dispositions
to handle affairs.

就 死 在 五 行 里 哦 ！
jiu si zai wu xing li o!
That is dying inside the Five Elements![15]

今 生 是 什 么 性 ，
jin sheng shi shen me xing,
If you know the Nature of this lifetime,

就 知 道 前 生 是 做 什 么 的 。
jiu zhi dao qian sheng shi zuo shen me de.
then you will know what you did
in the previous life.

今 生 是 火 性 ，
jin sheng shi huo xing,
If this life is of Fire Nature,

前 生 一 定 是 当 官 的 ；
qian sheng yi ding shi dang guan de;
in the previous life one certainly was an official.

今 生 是 水 性，

jin sheng shi shui xing,

If this life is of Water Nature,

前 生 一 定 是 商 人；

qian sheng yi ding shi shang ren;

in the previous life one certainly was a merchant.

今 生 是 木 性，

jin sheng shi mu xing,

If this life is of Wood Nature,

前 生 一 定 是 工 人；

qian sheng yi ding shi gong ren;

in the previous life one certainly was a laborer.

今 生 是 土 性，

jin sheng shi tu xing,

If this life is of Earth Nature,

前 生 一 定 是 庄 稼 人；

qian sheng yi ding shi zhuang jia ren;

in the previous life one certainly was a peasant.

今 生 是 金 性，

jin sheng shi jin xing,

If this life is of Metal Nature,

前生一定是读书人。

qian sheng yi ding shi mai shu ren.

in the previous life one certainly was a book seller.

前生好打猎或好杀害生灵的,

qian sheng hao da lie huo hao sha hai sheng ling de,

People who in the previous life were fond
of hunting or killing living souls,

今生火性就高。

jin sheng huo xing jiu gao.

in this life, the Fire Nature is therefore high.

前生好抗上的,

qian sheng hao kang shang de,

People who in the previous life
were fond of contradicting,

今生木性就大。

jin sheng mu xing jiu da.

in this life, the Wood-Nature is great.

前生好说谎的,

qian sheng hao shuo huang de,

People who in the previous life were fond of lying,

今生金性就强。

jin sheng jin xing jiu qiang.

in this life, the Metal-Nature is then strong.

前 生 好 怨 人 的 ，

qian sheng hao yuan ren de,

People who in the previous life were fond of grudges,

今 生 土 性 就 厚 。

jin sheng tu xing jiu hou.

in this life, the Earth Nature is dense.

达 天 时 是 阳 火 ，

da tian shi shi yang huo,

Attaining Heaven's Natural Order[16] is Yang Fire.

信 因 果 是 阳 土 ，

xin yin guo shi yang tu,

Believing in Cause and Effect is Yang Earth.

找 好 处 是 阳 金 ，

zhao hao chu shi yang jin,

Seeking positives is Yang Metal.

认 不 是 是 阳 水 ，

ren bu shi shi yang shui,

Admitting faults is Yang Water.

能 受 气 是 真 阳 木 ，

neng shou qi shi zhen yang mu,

Being able to endure bullying is true Yang Wood.

这 是 真 五 行 。

zhe shi zhen wu xing.

These are the true Five Elements.

现 今 的 天 时 ,

xian jin de tian shi,

In today's Natural Order of Heaven,

人 人 性 里 都 有 火 。

ren ren xing li dou you huo.

every human has Fire inside their Nature.

火 性 人 主 贪 、

huo xing ren zhu tan,

Fire-Natured people are governed by greed

好 争 理 ,

hao zheng li,

and are fond of arguing reason.

所 以 才 争 贪 不 已 、

suo yi cai zheng tan bu yi,

Therefore arguments and greed are endless,

战 乱 不 息 ,

zhan luan bu xi,

and chaotic wars ceaseless.

不 争 不 贪 是 真 阳 火 ，
bu zheng bu tan shi zhen yang huo,
Being without argument and greed is true Yang Fire.

真 阳 火 才 能 达 天 时
zhen yang huo cai neng da tian shi
Only True Yang Fire can attain
Heaven's Natural Order

（ 达 天 时 不 争 不 贪 ）。
(da tian shi bu zheng bu tan).
(Attainment of Heaven's Natural Order
is without argument and without greed.)

The Dao of striving for gracious balance

（五）

Chapter 5

三界

San Jie

The Three Realms

人是三界众生的，
ren shi san jie zhong sheng de,
People are amongst all living creatures
of the Three Realms,

天赋人的性，
tian fu ren de xing,
Heavenly gifted with Human Inner Nature,

地赋人的命，
di fu ren de ming,
Earthly gifted with Human Life-Destiny,

父母生的身，
fu mu sheng de shen,
and a Body born from a father and mother.

所以说三界是人的来踪。
suo yi shuo san jie shi ren de lai zong.
Therefore it is said that humans bear
the traces of the Three Realms.

性存天理，
xing cun tian li,
Inner Nature upholds the Principles of Heaven.

心存道理，
xin cun dao li,
The Heart upholds the Principles of the Dao.

身 尽 情 理 ，
shen jin qing li,
The Body puts to best use the Principles of Reason.

才 能 返 本 归 根 。
cai neng fan ben gui gen.
only then can one revert to one's Root
and return to the Source.

人 只 知 有 个 身 我 ，
ren zhi zhi you ge shen wo,
People only know there is a Body "I."[17]

不 知 天 上 有 个 性 我 ，
bu zhi tian shang you ge xing wo,
they do not know that in Heaven
there is an Inner Nature "I."

地 府 有 个 命 我 ，
di fu you ge ming wo,
and in the Earthly Mansions
there is a Life-Destiny "I."

性 化 了 ，
xing hua le,
When the Inner Nature is transformed,

天 上 的 性 我 得 天 爵 。
tian shang de xing wo de tian jue.
The Heavenly Nature "I" gains Heavenly Rank.

道 理 明 了 ，

dao li ming le,

Once the Principles of the Dao are understood,

地 府 的 命 我 得 人 爵 。

di fu de ming wo de ren jue.

the Life-Destiny "I" in the Earthly Mansions
gains Human Rank.

所 以 一 人 本 有 三 身 ，

suo yi yi ren ben you san shen,

Therefore a Human originally has Three Bodies,

可 惜 人 都 不 知 道 呀 ！

ke xi ren dou bu zhi dao ya!

it is pitiful that no one knows though!

我 所 讲 的 『 性 存 天 理 、

wo suo jiang de "xing cun tian li,

I talk about "Inner Nature,
which upholds the Principles of Heaven,

心 存 道 理 、

xin cun dao li,

The Heart, which upholds the Principles of the Dao,

身 尽 情 理 。』

shen jin qing li."

and the Body, which puts to best use
the Principles of Reason."

和 佛 家 的 三 皈 、
he fo jia de san gui,
With the Buddhist Three Refuges,

道 家 的 三 华 、
dao jia de san hua,
with the Three Flowers of Daoism,

儒 家 的 三 纲 是 一 样 的 。
ru jia de san gang shi yi yang de.
and with the Three Cardinal Rules
of Confucianism, they are identical.

佛 家 的 三 皈 就 是 性 、 心 、 身 。
fo jia de san gui jiu she xing, xin, shen.
The Buddhists' Three Refuges
are Inner Nature, Heart, and Body.

性 存 天 理 就 是 皈 依 佛 ,
xing cun tian li jiu shi gui yi fo,
Inner Nature upholding the Principles of Heaven,
is taking refuge in Buddha.

心 存 道 理 就 是 皈 依 法 ,
xin cun dao li jiu shi gui yi fa,
The Heart upholding the Principles of the Dao,
is taking refuge in the Dharma.

身 尽 情 理 就 是 皈 依 僧 。

shen jin qing li jiu shi gui yi seng.

The Body putting to best use the Principles of Reason,
is taking refuge in the Sangha.

道 家 的 三 华 就 是 性 、 心 、 身 。

dao jia de san hua jiu shi xing, xin, shen.

The Daoist Three Flowers are Inner Nature,
Heart, and Body.

性 华 开 天 理 足 ,

xing hua kai tian li zu,

When the Flower of Inner Nature blossoms,
the Principles of Heaven are fulfilled.

心 华 开 道 理 足 ,

xin hua kai dao li zu,

When the Heart-Flower blossoms,
the Principles of the Dao are fulfilled.

身 华 开 情 理 足 。

shen hua kai qing li zu.

When the Body-Flower blossoms,
the Principles of Reason are fulfilled.

儒 家 的 三 达 德 就 是 性 、 心 、 身 。

ru jia de san da de jiu shi xing, xin, shen.

The Confucian Three Virtues are exactly
Inner Nature, Heart and Body.

性 存 天 理 有 仁 ，
xing cun tian li you ren,
When Inner Nature upholds
the Principles of Heaven, there is benevolence,

心 存 道 理 有 智 ，
xin cun dao li you zhi,
When the Heart upholds the Principles of the Dao,
there is wisdom.

身 尽 情 理 要 蔼 和 。
shen jin qing li yao ai he.
When the Body puts to best use the
Principles of Reason, there shall be amiability.

性 要 服 人 ，
xing yao fu ren,
Inner Nature shall serve people.

不 服 人 伤 性 。
bu fu ren shang xing.
Not serving people will harm one's Inner Nature.

心 要 爱 人 ，
xin yao ai ren,
The Heart shall love people.

不 爱 人 伤 心 。
bu ai ren shang xin.
Not loving people harms the Heart.

身要让人，

shen yao rang ren,

The Body shall yield to people.

不让人伤身 。

bu rang ren shang shen.

Not yielding to people harms the Body.

性、心、身三界不太平，

xing, xin, shen san jie bu tai ping,

If Inner Nature, Heart, Body and the Three Realms
are not in great peace,

是因为三界中有三个贼，

shi yin wei san jie zhong you san ge zei,

it is because in the Three Realms
there are Three Thieves:

一禀性

yi bing xing

First, Natural Dispositions;

（又名气禀性，指怒、恨、怨、恼、烦而言），

(you ming qi bing xing, zhi nu, hen, yuan, nao, fan er yan),

(also called Qi-Disposition referring to wrath,
hatred, resentment, annoyance, and vexation).

二私欲，

er si yu,

Second, selfish desires;

三 不 良 嗜 好 。

san bu liang shi hao.

Third, unkind habits.

要 想 三 界 太 平 ,

yao xiang san jie tai ping,

Wishing the Three Realms to be in great peace,

就 要 用 天 理 捉 拿 性 中 的 贼 ,

jiu yao yong tian li zhuo na xing zhong de zei,

one must resort to the Principles of Heaven
to catch the Thief in one's Nature,

用 道 理 捉 拿 心 里 的 贼 ,

yong dao li zhuo na xin li de zei,

resort to the Principles of the Dao
to catch the Thief in one's Heart,

用 情 理 捉 拿 身 上 的 贼 。

yong qing li zhuo na shen shang de zei.

and resort to the Principles of Reason
to catch the Thief in one's Body.

三 皇 是 天 皇 、 地 皇 、 人 皇 ,

san huang shi tian huang, di huang, ren huang,

The Three Emperors are the Heavenly Emperor,
the Earthly Emperor and the Human Emperor.

人 说 是 上 古 的 三 位 皇 帝 ，
ren shuo shi shang gu de san wei huang di,
People say they are the ancient Three Sovereigns.

我 说 天 皇 是 玉 皇 爷 ，
wo shuo tian huang shi yu huang ye,
I say the Heavenly Emperor is the Jade Emperor,

管 人 的 性 ，
guan ren de xing,
ruling over Human Inner Nature.

人 要 是 动 性 耍 脾 气 ，
ren yao shi dong xing shua pi qi,
If people stir their Inner Nature and show bad temper,

天 就 降 灾 ；
tian jiu jiang zai;
Heaven will fall into calamity.

地 皇 是 阎 王 爷 ，
di huang shi yan wang ye,
The Earthly Emperor is Yama, the King of Hell,

管 人 的 命 ，
guan ren de ming,
ruling over Human Life-Destiny.

人要是坏了良心，

ren yao shi huai le liang xin,

If people spoil their conscience

违背伦常道，

wei bei lun chang dao,

and violate the Dao of Human Relationships,

地府就降病；

di fu jiu jiang bing;

the Earthly Mansions then will fall into sickness.

人皇是皇王爷，

ren huang shi huang wang ye,

The Human Emperor is the The Royal Emperor,

管人的身，

guan ren de shen,

ruling over the Human Body.

人要是犯罪，

ren yao shi fan zui,

If people commit offenses,

国法处罚。

guo fa chu fa.

they will be punished by the laws of the land.

三皇管人的性心身三界，

san huang guan ren de xing xin shen san jie,

The Three Emperors rule over the Three Realms
of the Human Inner Nature, Heart, and Body.

是为了叫人学好。

shi wei le jiao ren xue hao.

This is for the sake of teaching people
to emulate goodness.

心里心思别人不对是心病，

xin li xin si bie ren bu dui shi xin bing,

In your Heart, thoughts of other people
being wrong is sickness of the Heart.

性里常发脾气是性病，

xing li chang fa pi qi shi xing bing,

In your Inner Nature, constantly losing temper
is illness of the Inner Nature.

心病必引起性病，

xin bing bi yin qi bing xing,

Sickness of the Heart will certainly lead
to illness of the Inner Nature.

性病必引起身病，

xing bing bi yin qi shen bing,

Illness of the Inner Nature will certainly lead
to diseases of the Body.

能 反 过 来 病 就 好 了 。
neng fan guo lai bing jiu hao le.
If one can reverse disease, then all will be good.

性 界 清 没 有 脾 气 ,
xing jie qing mei you pi qi,
When Inner Nature is pure, there is no loss of temper.

心 界 清 没 有 私 欲 ,
xin jie qing mei you si yu,
When the Heart is pure, there are no selfish desires.

身 界 清 没 有 不 良 嗜 好 。
shen jie qing mei you bu liang shi hao.
When the Body is pure, there are no unkind habits.

性 不 清 没 有 福 ,
xing bu qing mei you fu,
When the Inner Nature is impure,
there is no good fortune.

心 不 清 没 有 禄 ,
xin bu qing mei you lu,
When the Heart is impure, there is no wealth.

身 不 清 没 有 寿 ,
shen bu qing mei you shou,
When the Body is impure, there is no longevity.

所 以 要 清 三 界 。

suo yi yao qing san jie.

Therefore one shall purify the Three Realms.

三 界 的 病 我 全 会 治 ，

san jie de bing wo quan hui zhi,

All of the sicknesses of the Three Realms
can be cured by the "I."

必 须 分 开 三 界 、

bi xu fen kai san jie,

It is necessary to part with the Three Realms

清 理 三 曹 。

qing li san cao.

and purify the Three Divisions.[18]

身 无 不 良 嗜 好 ，

shen wu bu liang shi hao,

When the Body is without unkind habits,

身 界 就 没 病 ；

shen jie jiu mei bing;

the Body Realm is without disease.

心 无 私 欲 ，

xin wu si yu,

When the Heart is without selfish desires,

心 界 就 没 病 ；

xin jie jiu mei bing;

the Heart Realm is without sickness.

性 无 脾 气 ，

xing wu pi qi,

When the Inner Nature is without bad temper,

性 界 就 没 病 。

xing jie jiu mei you bing.

the Inner Nature Realm is without illness.

心 性 的 病 ，

xin xing de bing

Disorders of the Heart and Inner Nature

非 用 道 治 不 好 ，

fei yong dao zhi bu hao,

are hard to cure without using the Dao.

吃 药 是 没 效 的 ，

chi yao shi mei xiao de,

Taking medicine is ineffective,

可 惜 人 都 不 知 道 呀 ！

ke xi ren dou bu zhi dao ya!

it is a pity that no one knows!

人 生 要 道 就 是 去 贪 、
ren sheng yao dao jiu shi qu tan,
When a Human in this life studies and cultivates
the path of the Dao, this removes greed,

去 争 、
qu zheng,
removes arguments,

去 搅 ,
qu rao,
and removes annoyance.

贪 的 亏 天 理 ,
tan de kui tian li,
Greedy people lack Principles of Heaven,

欠 天 上 债 ;
qian tian shang zhai;
owing Heavenly Debts.

争 的 亏 道 理 ,
zheng de kui dao li,
People who argue, lack the Principles of the Dao,

欠 人 间 债 ;
qian ren jian zhai;
owing Human Debts.

搅 的 亏 情 理 ，

jiao de kui qing li,

Disturbing people lack the Principles of Reason,

欠 阴 间 债 。

qian yin jian zhai.

owing Netherworldly Debts.

倘 若 三 个 字 都 犯 了 ，

tang ruo san ge zi dou fan le,

Supposing all three offenses are committed,

欠 三 界 的 债 ，

qian san jie de zhai,

owing debts to all Three Realms,

那 能 有 好 结 果 ？

na neng you hao jie guo?

how could this possibly lead to a good outcome?

贪 就 是 过 ，

tan jiu shi guo,

Greed is then the result,

争 就 是 罪 ，

zheng jiu shi zui,

arguments are then the offense,

搅 就 是 孽 。

jiao jiu shi nie.

disturbances are then the wrongdoing.

好 抱 屈 伤 心 ,

hao bao qu shang xin,

Being fond of bearing grudges harms the Heart.

不 抱 屈 保 气 保 命 。

bu bao qu bao qi bao ming.

Not bearing grudges protects Qi
and protects Life-Destiny.

好 后 悔 伤 性 ,

hao hou hui shang xing,

Being fond of regrets harms the Inner Nature.

不 后 海 保 性 保 福 。

bu hou hui bao xing bao fu.

Not having regrets protects one's Inner Nature
and protects one's good fortune.

好 怨 人 伤 身 ,

hao yuan ren shang shen,

Being fond of resenting people harms the Body.

不 怨 人 保 身 保 寿 。

bu yuan ren bao shen bao shou.

Not resenting people protects one's Body
and protects one's longevity.

人能不抱屈、

ren neng bao qu,

If people are able to not bear grudges,

不后悔、

bu hou hui,

not have regrets,

不怨人，

bu yuan ren,

and not resent people,

三界就都不受伤了。

san jie jiu dou bu shou shang le.

none of the Three Realms will sustain any harm.

我也有个三省，

wo ye you ge san xing.

I also have Three Introspections:

一省性中有没有脾气？

yi xing xing zhong you mei you pi qi?

First introspection, inside one's Inner Nature,
is there any bad temper?

有人拂逆我的时候，

you ren fu ni wo de shi hou,

When people go against me,

121

我 的 性 理 起 什 么 作 用 ？
wo de xing li qi shen me zuo yong?
in my Inner Nature, what effect is brought upon?

二 省 心 里 知 不 知 足 ？
er xing xin li zhi bu zhi zu?
Second introspection, in my Heart
do I know contentment?

有 没 有 偏 私 ？
you mei you pian si?
Is there any partiality or favoritism?

吃 亏 的 时 候 ，
chi kui de shi hou,
When suffering losses,

心 里 是 什 么 滋 味 ？
xin li shi shen me zi wei
in my Heart, what taste does it leave?

三 省 行 为 正 不 正 当 ？
san xing xing wei zheng bu zheng dang?
Third introspection, is my conduct
upright and proper or not?

确 实 会 做 什 么 ？
que shi hui zuo shen me?
Truly, what can be done?

这 就 是 我 的 三 省 。

zhe jiu shi wo de san xing.

These are therefore my Three Introspections.

我 也 有 个 三 纲 领 ，

wo ye you ge san gang ling,

I also have Three Guidelines:

就 是 性 存 天 理 ，

jiu shi xing cun tian li,

Inner Nature upholding the
Principles of Heaven,

心 存 道 理 ，

xin cun dao li,

the Heart upholding the Principles of the Dao,

身 尽 情 理 。

shen jin qing li.

and the Body putting to best use the
Principles of Reason.

我 也 有 个 八 条 目 ，

wo ye you ge ba tiao mu,

I also have Eight Clauses:

一 不 贪 、

yi bu tan,

First, no greed;

二 不 争、

er bu zheng,

Second, no arguments;

三 不 抱 屈、

san bu bao qu;

Third, no grudges.

四 不 后 悔、

si bu hou hui,

Fourth, no regrets.

五 不 怨 人、

wu bu yuan ren,

Fifth, no resentment towards people.

六 不 着 急、

liu bu zhao ji,

Sixth, no anxiety.

七 不 上 火、

qi bu shang huo,

Seventh, no flaring up of Fire.

八 不 生 气。

ba bu sheng qi.

Eighth, no raising of Qi.

若 能 做 到 ，
ruo neng zuo dao,
If it can be achieved,

不 费 金 钱 、
bu fei jin qian,
then there is no expense of money,

不 费 力 气 ，
bu fei li qi,
and no expense of effort.

不 但 成 道 ，
bu dan cheng dao,
One will not only realize the Dao,

还 能 成 佛 。
hai neng cheng fo.
but also attain Buddhahood.

人 有 三 宝 就 是 性 、 心 、 身 。
ren you san bao jiu shi xing, xin, shen.
Humans have Three Treasures:
Inner Nature, Heart, and Body.

性 属 水 、
xing shu shui,
Inner Nature belongs to Water.

心 属 火 、
xin shu huo,
The Heart belongs to Fire.

身 属 土 。
shen shu tu.
and the Body belongs to Earth.

水 是 人 的 精 ,
shui shi ren de jing.
Water is the Essence of Humans,

土 是 人 的 气 ,
tu shi ren de qi,
Earth is the Qi of Humans,

火 是 人 的 神 。
huo shi ren de shen.
and Fire is Spirit of Humans.

精 足 有 智 慧 、
jing zu you zhi hui,
Once Essence is ample,
one is endowed with wisdom.

气 足 有 发 育 、
qi zu you fa yu,
Once Qi is ample, there is growth
and development.

神 足 有 灵 。
shen zu you ling.
Once Spirit is ample, there is Divinity.

像 烧 砖 似 的 ,
xiang shao zhuan si de,
As if baking bricks,

先 用 土 坯 ,
xian yong tu pi,
first use earth bricks.

再 用 火 烧 ,
zai yong huo shao,
Then apply fire for baking.

最 后 用 水 浇 ,
zui hou yong shui jiao,
Last utilize water for sprinkling.

才 能 坚 固 。
cai neng jian gu.
Only then can they be solid.

大 家 讲 性 心 身 ,
da jia jiang xing xin shen,
Everyone discusses Inner Nature,
Heart, and Body.

讲几遍就等于烧几把火。

jiang ji bian jiu deng yu shao ji ba huo.

Discussing it several times is equal to baking
them in several rounds of Fire.

讲透了『三宝』足，

jiang tou le [san bao] zu,

When the "Three Treasures" are explained
and penetrated thoroughly,

胜享百官之富。

sheng xiang bai guan zhi fu.

there is enjoyment of the riches
of a Hundred Officials.[19]

能忍则性了，

neng ren ze xing le,

Being able to endure follows Inner Nature,

知足则心了，

zhi zu ze xin le,

knowing contentment follows the Heart

勤劳则身了，

qin lao ze shen le,

and being hardworking follows the Body.

这正是好了。

zhe zheng shi hao le.

This is truly good.

不 能 了 ，
bu neng le,
If one is incapable of doing it,

就 好 不 了 。
jiu hao bu liao.
then goodness is unachievable.

Equilibrium of the Three Realms

（六）

Chapter 6

三 性

San Xing

The Three
Inner Natures

人 有 三 性 、
ren you san xing,
People have Three Natures:

一 天 性 、
yi tian xing,
First, Heavenly Nature;

二 禀 性 ,
er bing xing,
Second, Endowed Nature;

三 习 性 。
san xi xing.
Third, Acquired Nature.

天 性 是 纯 善 无 恶 的 ,
tian xing shi chun shan wu e de,
The Heavenly Nature is pure,
benevolent and without evil.

孟 子 说 的 性 善 ,
meng zi shuo de xing shan,
The innate goodness that Mencius[20] speaks about,

正 是 指 的 天 性 。
zheng shi zhi de tian xing.
refers precisely to the Heavenly Nature.

人 赋 的 性 叫 禀 性 ，
ren fu de xing jiao bing xing,
The Nature that is bestowed upon people
is the Endowed Nature.

禀 性 是 纯 恶 无 善 的 ，
bing xing shi chun e wu shan de,
The Endowed Nature is purely wicked and malevolent.

荀 子 主 张 的 性 恶 ，
xun zi zhu zhang de xing e,
The Innate Wickedness that Xun Zi[21] proposes

正 是 指 的 禀 性 。
zheng shi zhi shi bing xing,
refers precisely to the Endowed Nature.

后 添 的 性 叫 习 性 ，
hou tian de xing jiao xi xing,
The last Nature is called the Acquired Nature.

习 性 是 可 善 可 恶 的 ，
xi xing shi ke shan ke e de,
The Acquired Nature could be good or evil,

『 近 朱 则 赤 ，
"jin zhu ze chi,
"Entering cinnabar, one is stained red,

135

近 墨 则 黑 。』

jin mo ze hei."

entering ink, one is stained black."

告 子 说 的 性

gao zi shuo de xing

The Nature that Gao Zi[22] discusses

『 可 东 可 西 』 正 是 指 的 习 性 。

"ke dong ke xi" zheng shi zhi de xi xing.

"Perhaps to the East, perhaps to the West,"[23]
refers to Acquired Nature.

以 天 性 用 事 的 会 找 人 好 处 ,

yi tian xing yong shi de hui zhao ren hao chu,

People resorting to the Heavenly Nature
to manage affairs will seek people's positives.

以 禀 性 当 家 的 准 看 人 不 对 。

yi bing xing dang jia de zhun kan ren bu dui.

People resorting to Endowed Nature for household affairs,
accordingly, see people's wrongdoings.

这 叫 什 么 性 ,

zhe jiao shen me xing,

What are these Natures called?

招 什 么 事 。

zhao shen me shi.

What matters do they beckon?

天 性 有 源 ，

tian xing you yuan,

Heavenly Nature has a source.

禀 性 有 根 。

bing xing you gen.

Endowed Nature has a root.

前 生 的 习 性 ，

qian sheng de xi xing,

Acquired Nature comes from previous lives

就 是 今 生 的 禀 性 。

jiu shi jin sheng de bing xing.

and is this life's Endowed Nature.

能 化 去 禀 性

neng hua qu bing xing

If one is able to transform and remove
the Endowed Natural Dispositions

（怒 、 恨 、 怨 、 恼 、 烦 ），

(nu,[24] hen, yuan, nao, fan),

(wrath, hatred, resentment, annoyance, and vexation),

天 性 就 圆 满 了 。

tian xing jiu yuan man le.

then Heavenly Nature is perfect in its circularity.

不 能 化 的 ，

bu neng hua de,

People who are unable to transform and remove them,

一 触 即 发 ，

yi chu ji fa,

once touched, they stir into existence,

像 被 鬼 迷 住 了 似 的 ，

xiang bei gui mi zhu le si e,

it is as if possessed by ghosts.

所 以 叫 做 『 五 鬼 』，

suo yi jiao zuo "wu gui,"

That is the reason why they are called "the Five Ghosts"

闹 得 家 宅 不 安 。

nao de jia zhai bu an.

and they stir up the domain of the home into unrest.

又 叫 做 『 五 毒 』，

you jiao zuo "wu du,"

They are also called "the Five Poisons."

令 人 害 病 死 亡 。

jin ren hai bing si wang.

People of today fall sick and die from them.

它 的 根 最 深 ,
ta de gen zui shen,
Their roots are the deepest,

不 易 拔 除 。
bu yi ba chu.
as it is not easy to pull them out.

人 若 是 降 伏 不 住 它 ,
ren ruo shi xiang fu bu zhu ta,
If people are unable to subdue them,

就 难 当 好 人 。
jiu nan dang hao ren.
it is hard to be a good person.

佛 说 :
fo shuo:
Buddha says:

『 业 力 随 身 ,
"ye li sui shen,
"If demonic forces follow the Body,

必 至 妄 动 无 明 。』
bi zhi wang dong wu ming."
certainly there will be rash actions out of ignorance."

难 以 成 道 。

nan yi cheng dao.

This makes it difficult to achieve the Dao.

习 性 是 物 欲 所 绕 ，

xi xing shi wu yu suo rao,

Acquired Nature revolves around materialistic desires.

禀 性 是 人 间 的 烦 恼 。

bing xing shi ren jian de fan nao.

The Endowed Natural Dispositions are the vexation
and agony of people's relations.

能 在 道 德 场 中 尽 义 务 ，

neng zai dao de chang zhong jin yi wu,

If one is able to work for no reward[25]
in the field of the Way and Virtue,

身 界 算 是 脱 出 去 了 。

shen jie suan shi tuo chu qu le.

the Human Realm is considered cast away.

会 当 人 的 ，

hui dang ren de,

If one is able to act as a good person,

脱 出 了 心 界 。

tuo chu le xin jie,

one casts off the Heart Realm.

禀性化尽，

bing xing hua jin,

Only when Endowed Nature is completely transformed

才脱出了性界。

cai tuo chu le xing jie.

is one able to shed the Nature Realm.

不然怎能『超出界外』呢？

bu ran zen neng "chao chu jie wai" ne?

Otherwise, how could one
"Transcend Beyond the Realms?"

神足即是德，

shen zu ji shi de,

The Spirit being ample is Virtue.

神足就乐，

shen zu jiu le,

The Spirit being ample is Joy.

乐就可以化禀性。

le jiu ke yi hua bing xing.

Joy then is able to transform the Endowed Nature.

脾气化尽，

pi qi hua jin,

When flaring tempers are completely transformed,

因 果 自 了 。

yin guo zi liao.

Cause and Effect will naturally abate.

去 习 性 、

qu xi xing,

Remove Acquired Nature,

化 禀 性 、

hua bing xing,

transform Endowed Nature,

圆 满 天 性 。

yuan man tian xing.

and make Heavenly Nature
perfect in its circularity.

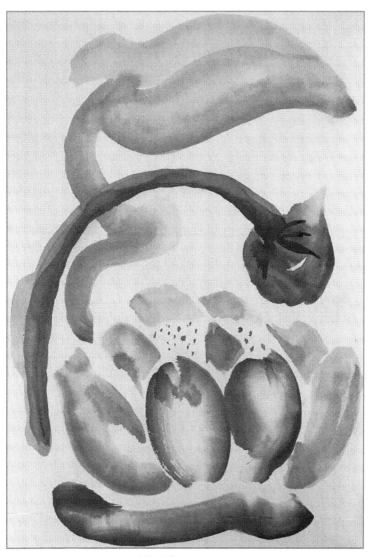

The Three Natures

（七）

Chapter 7

三命

San Ming

The Three Life-Destinies

人 有 三 命 ，

ren you san ming,

Humans have three Life-Destinies:

一 天 命 、

yi tian ming,

One, Heavenly Destiny;

二 宿 命 、

er su ming,

Two, Karmic Destiny;

三 阴 命 。

san yin ming.

Three, Yin Destiny.

性 与 天 命 合 ，

xing yu tian ming he,

Inner Nature and Heavenly Destiny are joined.

道 义 就 是 天 命 。

dao yi jiu shi tian ming.

Morality and justice are exactly Heavenly Destiny.

心 与 宿 命 合 ，

xin yu su ming he,

The Heart and Karmic Destiny are joined.

知 识 、
zhi shi,
Knowledge,

能 力 、
neng li,
ability,

钱 财 都 是 宿 命 。
qian cai dou shi su ming.
and wealth are all Karmic Destiny.

身 与 阴 命 合 ,
shen yu yin ming he,
The Body and the Yin Destiny are joined.

禀 性（怒 、恨 、怨 、恼 、烦 ）
bing xing (nu, hen, yuan, nao, fan)
The Endowed Natural Dispositions
(wrath, hatred, resentment, agony, and vexation)

就 是 阴 命 。
jiu shi yin ming.
are exactly this Yin Destiny.

把 这 三 命 研 究 明 白 ,
ba zhe san ming yan jiu ming bai,
Research and grasp these three Life-Destinies.

你 若 用 好 命 ，

ni ruo yong hao ming,

If you apply these Life-Destinies well,

你 的 命 准 好 。

ni de ming zhun hao.

then your Life-Destiny will be granted goodness.

命 好 命 不 好 ，

ming hao ming bu hao,

Whether your Life-Destinies are good or not

在 乎 自 己 ，

zai hu zi ji,

lies with oneself.

那 用 算 命 呢 ？

na yong suan ming ne?

What would be the use of calculating
one's Life-Destiny?

『 不 知 命 无 以 为 君 子 』，

"bu zhi ming wu yi wei jun zi,"

"Not knowing about Life-Destiny,
one is unable to be a noble person,"

不 知 人 不 能 『 达 彼 岸 』。

bu zhi ren bu neng "da bi an."

not knowing people, one is unable
to "Reach the Other Shore."[26]

知 人 的 好 处 是 知 天 命，

zhi ren de hao chu shi zhi tian ming,

Knowing people's positives
is knowing Heavenly Destiny,

知 人 的 功 劳 是 知 宿 命，

zhi ren de gong lao shi zhi su ming,

knowing people's merits
is knowing Karmic Destiny

知 人 的 禀 性 是 知 阴 命。

zhi ren de bing xing shi zhi yin ming.

and knowing people's Natural Dispositions
is knowing Yin Destiny.

知 命 的 人 才 是 君 子，

zhi ming de ren cai shi jun zi,

Only people who know Life-Destiny
are noble people.

好 动 禀 性 （ 耍 脾 气 ） 消 天 命，

hao dong bing xing (shua pi qi) xiao tian ming,

Being fond of the Natural Dispositions
(flaring tempers) eliminates Heavenly Destiny.

好 生 怨 气 消 宿 命，

hao sheng yuan qi xiao su ming,

Being fond of giving rise to resentment
eliminates Karmic Destiny.

151

好 占 便 宜 长 阴 命 。

hao zhan bian yi zhang yin ming.

Being fond of taking unfair advantage
increases Yin Destiny.

天 命 小 ,

tian ming xiao,

If Heavenly Destiny is minute,

要 会 长 。

yao hui zhang.

if desired, it can grow.

宿 命 小 ,

su ming xiao,

If Karmic Destiny is minute,

要 会 增 。

yao hui zeng.

if desired, it can increase.

阴 命 大 ,

yin ming da,

If Yin Destiny is great,

要 会 消 。

yao hui xiao.

if desired, it can be removed.

命 小 要 会 长 ，

ming xiao yao hui zhang,

If Life-Destiny is minute,
if desired, it can grow.

命 大 要 会 守 ，

ming da yao hui shou,

If Life-Destiny is great, if willing,
it can be safeguarded.

就 是 『 天 权 在 手 』 。

jiu shi "tian quan zai shou."

This is exactly, "The Authority of Heaven
in Your Hand."

有 人 来 见 我 ，

you ren lai jian wo,

When people come to see me,

我 先 问 他 是 做 什 么 的 ？

wo xian wen ta shi zuo shen me?

I first ask them what they are doing,

就 知 道 他 的 天 命 有 多 大 。

jiu zhi dao ta de tian ming you duo da.

so that I know exactly how great
their Heavenly Destiny is.

再 问 他 的 家 业 和 境 况 ，

zai wen ta de jia ye he qing kuang,

Then I ask them about the family enterprise
and its situation,

就 知 道 他 的 宿 命 有 多 大 。

jiu zhi dao ta de su ming you duo da.

so that I know how great their Karmic Destiny is.

看 看 他 的 禀 性 大 小 ，

kan kan ta de bing xing da xiao,

I look at their Endowed Natural Dispositions
and whether they are large or small,

就 知 道 他 的 阴 命 大 小 。

jiu zhi dao ta de yin ming da xiao.

so that I know whether their Yin Destiny
is large or small.

三 命 是 三 界 ，

san ming shi san jie,

The Three Life-Destinies are the Three Realms.

三 界 贯 通 ，

san jie guan tong,

When the Three Realms are threaded together,

还 有 不 知 道 的 吗 ？

hai you bu zhi dao de ma?

what could still be unknown?

人 都 没 有 为 众 人 的 心 ，

ren dou mei you wei zhong ren de xin,

All people have no Heart for the masses

只 知 为 己 ，

zhi zhi wei ji,

and only know their own Self.

所 以 才 糟 的 ，

suo yi cai zao de,

That is why there are still people in a wretched state.

我 所 以 能 成 为 善 人 ，

wo suo yi neng cheng wei shan ren,

I am thus able to become a benevolent person

是 因 为 我 把 为 己 的 心 开 除 了 ，

shi yin wei wo ba wei ji de xin kai chu le,

because I expel the selfish Heart,

也 就 是 把 宿 命 掐 死 了 。

ye jiu shi ba su ming qia si le.

which is choking Karmic Destiny to death.

宿 命 是 无 尽 无 休 的 ，

su ming shi wu jin wu xiu de,

Karmic Destiny is inexhaustible and ceaseless.

155

为 它 还 有 头 吗 ?

wei ta hai you tou ma?

Is there an end to it?

孟 子 说 :

meng zi shuo:

Mencius says:

『 修 其 天 爵 而 人 爵 从 之 』.

"xiu qi tian jue er ren jue cong zhi."

"Cultivating the nobility of Heaven is also where the
nobility of Humanity comes from."

可 是 人 一 得 了 人 爵 ,

ke shi ren yi de le ren jue,

Yet, once people have achieved
the Human Rank of nobility,

就 不 再 修 天 爵 啦 !

jiu bu zai xiu tian jue la!

they do not continue to cultivate
the Heavenly Rank of nobility!

修 德 性 是 长 (音 掌) 天 命 。

xiu de xing shi zhang (yin zhang) tian ming.

Cultivating morality is to increase
the Heavenly Destiny.

学 习 技 艺 、
xue xi ji yi,
The study of skills and arts and

多 积 钱 财 ,
duo ji qian cai,
accumulating more riches

都 是 长 宿 命 。
dou shi zhang su ming.
are all increasing Karmic Destiny.

善 用 宿 命 的 长 （ 音 常 ） 知 足 ,
shan yong su ming de chang (yin chang) zhi zu,
People who are good at using Karmic Destiny
for benevolence know contentment

能 消 阴 命 。
neng xiao yin ming.
and are able to eliminate Yin Destiny.

不 会 用 的 长 阴 命 ,
bu hui yong de zhang yin ming,
People who are incapable of using it,
increase Yin Destiny.

只 有 长 天 命 ,
zhi you zhang tian ming,
Only people who increase Heavenly Destiny

是一定可以消阴命。

shi yi ding ke yi xiao yin ming.

will certainly eliminate Yin Destiny.

现今的人，

xian jin de ren,

People of today,

只知用阴命、

zhi zhi yong yin ming,

only knowing how to resort to Yin Destiny,

重宿命，

zhong su ming,

value Karmic Destiny.

不知道长天命，

bu zhi dao zhang tian ming,

Not knowing of increasing Heavenly Destiny,

又怎能明白天道呢？

you zen neng ming bai tian dao ne?

how could they understand the Heavenly Dao?

以宿命为公益的长天命，

yi su ming wei gong yi de zhang tian ming,

People who use Karmic Destiny for public welfare
increase Heavenly Destiny

以宿命为自己享受的长阴命。

yi su ming wei zi ji xiang shou de zhang yin ming.

and people using Karmic Destiny
for their own joy increase Yin Destiny.

所以说有钱会花超三界,

suo yi shuo you qian hui hua chao san jie,

Therefore it is said that having money, you will be able
to buy yourself out and beyond the Three Realms,

不会花的孽难逃。

bu hui hua de nie nan tiao.

however, the wrongdoings that cannot be paid off
are difficult to escape from.

香瓜,

xiang gua,

A fragrant muskmelon,

苦的时候正长（音掌）;

ku de shi hou zheng zhang (yin zhang);

at a time of bitterness, it truly develops.

天命,

tian ming,

Heavenly Destiny,

苦的时候也正长。

ku de shi hou zheng zhang.

at a time of bitterness, it truly develops.

不 说 人 的 不 对 ,

bu shuo ren de bu dui,

People who do not bring up other people's wrongdoings

是 消 阴 命 。

shi xiao yin ming.

eliminate Yin Destiny.

能 忍 才 可 以 消 阴 命 。

neng ren cai ke yi xiao yin ming.

If being able to endure, then one is able
to eliminate Yin Destiny.

若 能 忍 受 大 侮 辱 ,

ruo neng ren shou da wu ru,

If being able to endure greatest humiliation and insult,

便 消 许 多 阴 命 。

bian xiao xu duo yin ming.

then some of Yin Destiny is eliminated.

天 命 大 的 宿 命 也 不 小 ,

tian ming da de su ming ye bu xiao,

People with great Heavenly Destiny
also have a Karmic Destiny that is not minor.

宿 命 大 的 阴 命 了 不 了 。

su ming da de yin ming liao bu liao.

People whose Karmic Destiny is great
cannot bring an end to Yin Destiny.

所 以 要 止 宿 命、

suo yi yao zhi su ming,

Therefore you need to stop your Karmic Destiny,

了 阴 命、

liao yin ming,

finish your Yin Destiny

长 天 命。

zhang tian ming.

and increase your Heavenly Destiny.

Release of the Yin Destiny

（八）

Chapter 8

性 命 [27]

Xing Ming

Inner Nature &
Life-Destiny

性 命 是 人 的 根 ，
xing ming shi ren de gen,
Inner Nature and Life Destiny
are the roots of Humans.

我 得 到 了 人 跟 ，
wo de dao le ren gen,
I obtained the root of a Human

那 道 根 也 就 算 得 着 了 。
na dao gen ye jiu suan de zhao le.
and that also counts as having obtained
the root of the Dao.

道 根 是 人 的 性 ，
dao gen shi ren de xing,
The root of the Dao is the Inner Nature of Humans

人 根 是 人 的 命 ，
ren gen shi ren de ming,
and the Human root is the Life-Destiny of Humans.

性 根 若 是 好 了 ，
xing gen ruo shi hao le,
If the root of Inner Nature is good,

那 命 根 也 没 个 不 好 。
na ming gen ye mei ge bu hao.
then the root of Life-Destiny is without any wrongs.

可 见 人 的 命 不 好 ，
ke jian ren de ming bu hao,
On the contrary if you see a person with bad Life-Destiny,

都 是 被 性 子 累 的 。
dou shi bei xing zi ji de.
all of it is accumulated from Inner Nature.

所 以 我 教 人 性 命 ，
suo yi wo jiao ren xing ming,
That is the reason I teach people about
Inner Nature and Life-Destiny.

人 能 化 性 ，
ren neng hua xing,
When people are capable of the
transformation of Inner Nature,

就 算 得 道 。
jiu suan de dao.
this precisely counts as achieving the Dao.

性 是 命 的 根 ，
xing shi ming de gen,
Inner Nature is the root of Life-Destiny,

有 德 的 人 性 量 必 大 ，
you de de ren xing liang bi da,
People with Virtue have a relatively
great capacity of Inner Nature,

167

性 量 大 ,

xing liang da,

When Inner Nature is great,

命 也 必 大 。

ming ye bi da.

then Life-Destiny is also comparatively great.

人 的 命 都 是 好 命 ,

ren de ming dou shi hao ming,

If people's Life-Destiny is an all-around
good Life-Destiny,

因 为 性 子 不 好 ,

yin wei xing zi bu hao,

yet, their Inner Nature is bad,

把 命 也 拐 带 坏 啦 !

ba ming ye guai dai huai la!

it will abduct the Life-Destiny into wickedness!

性 是 根 ,

xing shi gen,

Inner Nature is the root,

命 是 果 ,

ming shi guo,

Life-Destiny is the fruit.

扎 下 根 才 能 结 果 。

zha xia gen cai neng jie guo.

Only with roots penetrating is one able to bear fruits.

人 若 是 定 不 住 性 ，

ren ruo shi ding bu zhu xing,

If people are unable to stabilize their Inner Nature,

就 是 没 扎 下 根 。

jiu shi mei zha xia gen.

it is because no roots have penetrated.

若 不 认 命 ，

ruo bu ren ming,

If not accepting of Life-Destiny,

也 难 结 果 ，

ye nan jie guo

it is also difficult to bear fruits.

好 似 开 个 幌 花 。

hao si kai ge huang hua.

It is like blossoming a false flower.

学 道 的 人 ，

xue dao de ren,

People who study the Dao:

一要化性，

yi yao hua xing,

One, they want to transform Inner Nature;

二要认命。

er yao ren ming.

Two, they want to accept Life-Destiny.

性化了就不生气，

xing hua le jiu bu sheng qi,

Once Inner Nature is transformed,
then there will be no raising of Qi,

不生气才肯吃亏，

bu sheng qi cai ken chi kui,

If one does not raise Qi,
then one is willing to suffer losses.

吃亏就是占便宜。

chi kui jiu shi zhan pian yi.

Suffering losses is to be in an advantageous position.

认命就不怨人，

ren ming jiu bu yuan ren,

Accepting Life-Destiny is not resenting people.

不怨人才能受苦，

bu yuan ren cai neng shou ku,

Only by not resenting people
is one able to endure bitterness.

受 苦 才 能 享 福 。

shou ku cai neng xiang fu.

Only by enduring bitterness
is one able to enjoy good fortune.

可 惜 世 人 都 不 知 道 ,

ke xi shi ren dou bu zhi dao,

It is a pity that all worldly people
do not know about this,

把 性 命 看 轻 ,

ba xing ming kan qing,

taking Inner Nature and Life-Destiny lightly,

把 名 利 看 重 啦 !

ba ming li kan zhong la!

while looking heavily upon fame and gain!

古 人 说 :

gu ren shuo:

The ancient people said:

『 修 命 不 修 性 ,

"xiu ming bu xiu xing,

"Cultivating Life-Destiny without
cultivating Inner Nature

此 是 修 行 第 一 病 ;

ci shi xiu xing di yi bing;

is the first error in cultivation;

修 性 不 修 命 ，
xiu xing bu xiu ming,
if one is cultivating Inner Nature
without cultivating Life-Destiny,

一 点 灵 光 无 处 用 。』
yi dian ling guang wu chu yong"
even a tiny speck of Divine Light
is without purpose at all."

这 话 把 性 命 变 修 的 重 要 ，
zhe hua ba xing ming bian xiu de zhong yao,
These words review the importance of Inner Nature
and Life-Destiny for transformation and cultivation.

说 得 太 透 彻 啦 ！
shuo de tai tou che la!
It is explained thoroughly and penetratingly clear!

Cultivation of the root for the fruit

(九)

Chapter 9

四大界

Si Da Jie

The Four Great Realms

志、

zhi,

Will,

意、

yi,

Intent,

心 、

xin,

Heart

身 四 大 界 （ 四 个 境 界 ）。

shen si da jie (si ge jing jie).

and Body, are the Four Great Realms
(Four Boundaries).

迷 信 的 人 说 ，

mi xin de ren shuo,

People in blind faith say that

奈 河 桥 上 三 条 路 ，

nai he qiao shang san tiao lu,

on the bridge of the River to Hell[28] are three roads.

一 条 是 金 ，

yi tiao shi jin,

one is Gold,

一条是银，

yi tiao shi yin,

one is Silver,

一条就是黄泉路。

yi tiao jiu shi huang quan lu.

one is the road to the Yellow Springs.[29]

我说用志做人就是『金』，

wo shuo yong zhi zuo ren jiu shi "jin,"

I say that resorting to Will to act
as Human is exactly "Gold."

用意做人就是『银』，

yong yi zuo ren jiu shi "yin,"

Resorting to Intent to act as Human is "Silver."

以身心用事，

yi shen xin yong shi,

Using one's Body and Heart to undertake affairs

就是走上了『黄泉路』。

jiu shi zou shang le "huang quan lu."

is exactly walking on the road of the "Yellow Springs."

我常说，

wo chang shuo,

I constantly say

一个人必须把四大界分别清楚。

yi ge ren bi xu ba si da jie fen bie qing chu.

a person must differentiate
the Four Great Realms very clearly.

究竟咋样算是分清呢？

jiu jing za yang suan shi fen qing ne?

Actually, what is considered a clear distinction?

若能本性如如不动

ruo neng ben xing ru ru bu dong

If one is able to get one's Natural Instincts
to Ultimate Reality and be non-stirring

（骂也不动性、

(ma ye bu dong xing,

(cursing, also not stirring one's Inner Nature;

打也不动性、

da ye bu dong xing,

fighting, also not stirring one's Inner Nature;

杀了也不动性），

sha le ye bu dong xing,

and killing, also not stirring one's Inner Nature),

把世间的愚人都托起来，

ba shi jian de yu ren dou tuo qi lai,

then prop up all fools of this world

使他们成为大智慧人，

shi ta men cheng wei da zhi hui ren,

and turn them into great Wisemen.

便是志界，

bian shi zhi jie,

Then one is in the Realm of Will.

就是佛国的境界。

jiu shi fo guo de jing jie.

This is exactly the Realm of the Buddha Land.

若能心无一物，

ruo neng xin wu yi wu,

If one is able to be without
a single matter in the Heart,

常乐无忧

chang le wu you,

if one is constantly in joy and without worries,

便是意界，

bian shi yi jie,

then one is in the Realm of Intent.

就是天堂的境界。

jiu shi tian tang de jing jie.

This is the Realm of the Heavenly Hall.

若 是 贪 得 无 厌，

ruo shi tan de wu yan,

If one's greed is insatiable

多 忧 多 虑，

duo you duo lü,

and there are many worries and many preoccupations,

便 是 心 界，

bian shi xin jie,

then one is in the Realm of the Heart.

就 是 苦 海 的 境 界。

jiu shi ku hai de jing jie.

This is the Realm of the Sea of Bitterness.

若 是 为 名 为 利，

ruo shi wei ming wei li,

If one is after fame and gain,

争 贪 搅 扰，

zheng tan jiao rao,

then arguments and greed will cause disturbances.

花 天 酒 地，

hua tian jiu di,

If chasing the Flowers of Heaven
and the Wines of Earth,[30]

流连忘返,

liu lian wang fan,

enjoying oneself so much as to forget to return,

好勇斗狠,

hao yong dou hen,

and if one is fond of bravery and combat,

便是身界,

bian shi shen jie,

this is the Realm of the Body

就是地狱的境界,

jiu shi di yu de jing jie,

and exactly the Realm of Hell.

所以说,

suo yi shuo,

Therefore it is said,

志界是佛国,

zhi jie shi fo guo,

the Realm of Will is the Buddha Land.

意界是天堂,

yi jie shi tian tang,

The Realm of Intent is the Heavenly Hall.

心 界 是 苦 海 ，

xin jie shi ku hai,

The Realm of Heart is the Sea of Bitterness.

身 界 是 地 狱 。

shen jie shi di yu.

The Realm of Body is Hell.

志 界 人 没 说 （没 有 说 道 ， 怎 样 都 好 ），

zhi jie ren mei shuo (mei you shuo dao, zen yang dou hao),

In the Realm of Will, people do not discuss
(not discussing, all is good anyway).

意 界 人 知 足 ，

yi jie ren zhi zu,

In the Realm of Intent,
people know contentment.

心 界 人 好 贪 ，

xin jie ren hao tan,

In the Realm of the Heart,
people are fond of greed.

身 界 人 好 斗 。

shen jie ren hao dou.

In the Realm of the Body,
people are fond of fighting.

没 说 的 叫 做 无 心 人 ,
mei shuo de jiao zuo wu xin ren,
People who do not discuss
are called Non-Hearted Humans,[31]

知 足 的 叫 做 净 心 人 ,
zhi zu de jiao zuo jing xin ren,
People with contentment
are called Pure-Hearted Humans.

好 贪 的 叫 做 操 心 人 ,
hao tan de jiao zuo cao xin ren,
People fond of greed
are called Trouble-Hearted Humans.

好 斗 的 叫 做 糟 心 人 。
hao dou de jiao zuo zao xin ren.
People fond of fighting
are called Wretch-Hearted Humans.

糟 心 人 是 鬼 ,
zao xin ren shi gui.
Wretch-Hearted people are Ghosts.

操 心 人 是 人 ,
cao xin ren shi ren,
Trouble-Hearted people are Humans.

净 心 人 是 神 ，

jing xin ren shi shen,

Pure-Hearted people are Spirits.

没 心 人 是 佛 。

mei xin ren shi fo.

Non-Hearted people are Buddhas.

身 界 人 只 知 为 身 子 做 打 算 ，

shen jie ren zhi zhi wei shen zi zuo da suan,

People of the Realm of the Body are only attending
to their base Body,[32]

有 己 无 人 ，

you ji wu ren,

just themselves, no one else.

横 不 讲 理 ，

heng bu jiang li,

They are unrestrained and without reason.

见 着 东 西 就 想 占 为 己 有 ，

jian zhe dong xi jiu xiang zhan wei ji you,

Upon seeing things, they at once think about
how to possess them for themselves.

占 不 到 便 宜 就 生 气 打 架 ，

zhan bu dao pian yi jiu sheng qi da jia,

When they are not in advantageous positions,
they at once raise their Qi and fight

总 是 发 愁，

zong shi fa chou,

and are always showing worry.

所 以 是 个 鬼 。

suo yi shi ge gui.

These are the reasons they are Ghosts.

心 界 人 贪 而 无 厌，

xin jie ren tan er wu yan,

People from the Realm of the Heart
are insatiably greedy,

总 是 不 知 足，

zong shi bu zhi zu,

never knowing contentment,

满 脑 子 妄 想，

man nao zi wang xiang,

their minds being completely filled
with delusional thoughts

好 用 机 谋 巧 算，

hao yong ji mou qiao suan,

and they are fond of using
schemes and clever strategies.

所 以 是 个 小 人 。

suo yi shi ge xiao ren.

These are the reasons they are lowly people.

意 界 人 知 足 常 乐 ，

yi jie ren zhi zu chang le,

People of the Realm of Intent
know contentment and are constantly in joy,

乐 就 是 『 神 』。

le jiu shi "shen."

and joy is exactly "Spirit."

志 界 人 一 切 没 说 ，

zhi jie ren yi qie mei shuo,

People from the Realm of the Will
do not discuss anything.

看 透 因 果 ，

kan tou yin guo.

They see clearly through Cause and Effect

不 找 循 环 ，

bu zhao xun huan,

and are not seeking to Cycle,[33]

没 说 就 是 『 佛 』。

mei shuo jiu shi "fo."

thus being without speaking
is the same as "Buddhahood."

人要想超凡入圣，

ren yao xiang chao fan ru sheng,

If people want to transcend the ordinary
and enter sagehood,

得会挪界（转移境界）。

de hui na jie (zhuan yi jie jing).

they must reach the ability to shift Realms
(transfer boundaries).

身界的人互相揭短，

shen jie de ren hu xiang jie duan ,

People from the Realm of the Body
mutually expose their flaws.

心界的人互相争理，

xin jie de ren hu xiang zheng li,

People from the Realm of the Heart
mutually argue reason.

意界的人互相容让，

yi jie de ren hu xiang rong rang,

People from the Realm of Intent
mutually yield and show lenience.

志界的人互相感恩。

zhi jie de ren hu xiang gan en.

People from the Realm of Will
mutually feel gratitude.

佛 界 人 不 思 而 得 ，

fo jie ren bu si er de,

People from the Buddha Realm
have nothing in mind and obtain something.

神 界 人 思 则 得 之 ，

shen jie ren si ze de zhi,

People from the Spirit Realm
thoughtfully ponder and therefore achieve.

魔 （ 心 ） 界 人 『 求 』 才 能 得 ，

mo (xin) jie ren "qiu" cai neng de,

People from the Demon (Heart) Realm
"seek," only then are they able to achieve.

鬼 （ 身 ） 界 人 『 争 』 才 能 的 。

gui (shen) jie ren "zheng" cai neng de.

People from the Ghost (Body) Realm
"contest" and only then can they achieve.

志 有 志 的 性 ，

zhi you zhi de xing,

The Will has its own Inner Nature

他 是 无 为 无 不 为 的 。

ta shi wu wei wu bu wei de.

and it is non-action and not non-action.[34]

意 有 意 的 性 ，

yi you yi de xing,

The Intent has its own Inner Nature.

是 信 着 人 的 ，

shi xin zhe ren de,

It is trust in people.

遇 着 好 事 就 愿 意 让 给 别 人 。

yu zhe hao shi jiu yuan yi rang gei bie ren.

Encountering good matters one is willing
to be allowing and giving to others.

心 有 心 的 性 ，

xin you xin de xing,

The Heart has its own Inner Nature,

他 是 贪 而 无 厌 ，

ta shi tan er wu yan,

it is insatiably greedy,

一 心 为 己 ，

yi xin wei ji,

wholeheartedly for the Self

总 想 占 人 的 便 宜 。

zong xiang zhan ren de pian yi.

and always thinking about being
in advantageous positions over people.

身 有 身 的 性 ，

shen you shen de xing,

The Body has its own Inner Nature.

他 是 破 坏 成 性 的 ，

ta shi po huai cheng xing de,

Destruction becomes its Inner Nature.

人 己 两 伤 也 不 知 悔 。

ren ji liang shang ye bu zhi hui.

After the Human Body and the Self are both injured,
it still does not know repentance.

所 以 说 ，

suo yi shuo,

Therefore, it is said,

心 身 两 界 ，

xin shen liang jie,

the Realms of the Heart and the Body

绝 不 可 叫 他 为 主 ，

jue bu ke jiao ta wei zhu,

are absolutely not to be summoned
to act as one's master.

只 可 叫 他 听 命 。

zhi ke jiao ta ting ming.

Only summon them to obey your orders.

讲 佛 经 的 人 说：

jiang fo jing de ren shuo:

People explaining the Buddha scriptures say that

人 死 之 后 要 入 六 道 轮 回 。

ren si zhi hou yao ru liu dao lun hui

after people die, they will enter
the Six Paths of the Wheel of Life.[35]

我 说 六 道 轮 回 ，

wo shuo liu dao lun hui,

I speak of the Six Paths of the Wheel of Life.

都 在 我 们 身 上 呢 ！

dou zai wo men shen shang ne!

They are all within our Bodies!

何 必 向 外 求 ？

he bi xiang wai qiu?

Why should they be sought on the outside?

人 的 持 身 行 事 ，

ren de chi shen xing shi,

If people are conducting themselves properly

用 志 的 便 是 人 道 ，

yong zhi de bian shi ren dao,

and if people are resorting to Will,
then it is the Dao of Humanity.

贪 取 外 物、

tan qu wai wu,

If people are coveting objects on the outside

不 顾 情 理 的 便 是 物 道 （指 畜 牲 道 ），

bu gu qing li de bian shi wu dao (zhi chu sheng dao),

and if people are ignoring the Principles of Reason,
then it is the Dao of Objects,
(referring to the Dao of Domesticated Animals),

专 好 上 火 的 便 是 妖 道 ,

zhuan hao shang huo de bian shi yao dao,

If people are being particularly prone to Flaring Fire, then it
is the Dao of Demons.

专 好 生 气 的 便 是 鬼 道 ,

zhuan hao sheng qi de bian shi gui dao,

If people are being particularly prone to raising Qi,
then it is the Dao of Ghosts.

这 六 道 每 天 都 轮 回 在 我 们 身 上 ,

zhe liu dao mei tian dou lun hui zai wo men shen shang,

Every day these Six Paths of the Wheel of Life
cycle inside our bodies.

何 必 等 死 后 呢 ?

he bi deng si hou ne?

Why should we wait till after death?

佛说有三千大千世界，

fo shuo you san qian da qian shi jie,

Buddha says there are
Three Thousand Boundless Realms.

我说有四个大世界，

wo shuo you si ge da shi jie,

I say there are Four Great Realms

得道的人一眼就看出是那一界的人。

de dao de ren yi yan jiu kan chu shi na yi jie de ren.

and people who have achieved the Dao can see clearly, with
one glimpse, which realm people are from.

以身当人的，

yi shen dang ren de,

People who resort to the Body to act as Humans,

不论做到什么地步也是个破败星。

bu lun zuo dao shen me di bu ye shi ge po bai xing.

regardless of what state they reach,
it is only a Ruined Star.[36]

以心当人的，

yi xin dang ren de,

People who resort to the Heart to act as Humans,

不论事情怎么能干，

bu lun shi qing zen me neng gan,

regardless of how they handle affairs,

也 是 个 操 心 人 ，

ye shi ge cao xin ren,

are also Trouble-Hearted Humans.

以 意 当 人 的 ，

yi yi dang ren de,

People who resort to Intent to act as Humans,

不 论 事 情 怎 么 多 ，

bu lun shi qing zen me duo,

regardless of how many issues there are,

也 不 累 心 ，

ye bu lei xin,

their Heart remains tireless.

是 位 活 神 仙 。

shi wei huo shen xian.

This is the status of a Living Spirit Immortal.

以 志 当 人 的 ，

yi zhi dang ren de,

People resorting to Will to act as Humans,

不 论 遇 着 多 么 逆 的 环 境 ，

bu lun yu zhe duo me ni de huan jing,

regardless of how many opposing environments
they encounter,

也不动性,

ye bu dong xing,

it never stirs their Inner Nature.

就是一尊佛。

jiu shi yi zun fo.

This is the same as the respected Buddha.

有所忧患则志倒,

you suo you huan ze zhi dao,

A certain degree of misery
means one's Will topples.

有所恐惧意倒,

you suo kong ju yi dao,

A certain degree of fear means one's Intent topples.

有所好乐则心不正,

you suo hao le ze xin bu zheng,

A certain degree of fondness of joy
means the Heart is not upright.

有所忿懥则身不正。

you suo fen zhi ze shen bu zheng.

A certain degree of fury
means the Body is not upright.

苦极生志,

ku ji sheng zhi,

Extreme bitterness gives birth to Will.

乐 极 生 意 ,

le ji sheng yi,

Extreme joy gives birth to Intent.

真 了 就 是 佛 ,

zhen le jiu shi fo,

If true and authentic, then it is a Buddha.

假 了 就 是 魔 。

jia le jiu shi mo.

If fake and false, then it is a Demon.

有 病 就 是 地 狱 ,

you bing jiu shi di yu,

Being afflicted by illnesses is exactly Hell.

贪 心 就 是 苦 海 。

tan xin jiu shi ku hai.

A Heart of Greed is exactly the Sea of Bitterness.

会 使 用 志 的 人 ,

hui shi yong zhi de ren,

For people who are able to employ their Will,

越 遇 逆 境 越 乐 。

yue yu ni jing yue le.

the more adverse the circumstances they meet,
the more in joy they are.

会 使 用 意 的 人 ，
hui shi yong yi de ren,
For people who are able to employ their Intent,

意 念 多 大 ，
yi nian duo da,
depending on how great their thoughts are,

义 气 也 多 大 。
yi qi ye duo da.
that is how great their spirit of justice is.

心 中 有 累 ，
xin zhong you lei,
If there are toils in the Heart,

就 是 命 中 有 累 ，
jiu shi ming zhong you lei,
then there are toils in the Life-Destiny.

事 实 上 必 有 累 事 。
shi shi shang bi you lei shi.
In fact there must be toils.

不 高 兴 是 生 心 眼 啦 ！
bu gao xing shi sheng xin yan la!
Unhappiness creates the Eye of the Heart.[37]

意像皮球似的，

yi xiang pi qiu si de,

When Intent is like a leather ball

有针鼻大小的眼，

you zhen bi da xiao de yan,

and there is a hole the size of the eye of a needle,

就漏气了！

jiu lou qi le!

it will consequently leak air!

性是本，

xing shi ben,

Inner Nature is the origin.

志是根，

zhi shi gen,

Will is the root.

是万事万物的根。

shi wan shi wan wu de gen.

It is the the root of the Ten Thousand Manifestations
and the Ten Thousand Things.

根想雨似的，

gen xiang yu si de,

The root is like rain.

天 雨 本 来 无 心 ，

tian yu ben lai wu xin,

The rains from Heaven are originally without Heart,

可 是 酸 梨 得 了 必 酸 ，

ke shi suan li de le bi suan,

yet the sour pear must certainly obtain sourness

甘 草 得 了 必 甜 ，

gan cao de le bi gan,

and yet sweet grass must certainly obtain sweetness.

志 在 天 地 之 间 ，

zhi zai tian di zhi jian,

When Will is amidst Heaven and Earth,

也 像 那 雨 一 样 。

ye xiang na yu yi yang.

it is also like that rain.

死 心 才 能 化 性 ，

si xin cai neng hua xing,

When the Heart dies, then one
will be able to transform one's Inner Nature.

禀 性 化 了 而 后 意 诚 ，

bing xing hua le er hou yi cheng,

After the Endowed Natural Dispositions
are transformed, the Intent is sincere.

意 诚 而 后 志 诚 ，

yi cheng er hou zhi cheng,

After Intent is sincere,

Will will become sincere.

这 是 一 定 的 道 理 。

zhe shi yi ding de dao li.

These are fixed Principles.

禀 性 化 了 就 是 意 ，

bing xing hua le jiu shi yi,

When the Endowed Natural Dispositions
are transformed, this is exactly Intent.

我 们 化 世 界 ，

wo men hua shi jie,

When we transform the world,

轻 则 用 意 ，

qing ze yong yi,

lightly means using Intent,

重 则 使 志 。

zhong ze shi zhi.

heavily means utilizing Will.

能 够 用 志 的 ，

neng gou yong zhi de,

People who are able to use Will

万 世 罪 孽 一 笔 勾 消 。
wan shi zui nie yi mao gou xiao.
write off the retributions of the Ten Thousand
Generations with one stroke of a brush.

可 是 魔 来 了 ,
ke shi mo lai le,
However, when Demons appear

你 可 得 定 住 ,
ni ke de ding zhu,
and you are capable of reaching stabilization,

稍 微 一 动 ,
shao wei yi dong,
with the slightest movement

便 是 种 子 。
bian shi zhong zi.
it then becomes a seed.[38]

把 一 切 假 事 看 破 ,
ba yi qie jia shi kan po,
See through all falsities

自 然 成 真 。
zi ran cheng zhen.
and you will naturally realize the Truth.

天 堂 没 有 坏 人 ，

tian tang mei you huai ren,

There are no wicked people in the Heavenly Hall.

地 狱 没 有 好 人 ，

di yu mei you hao ren,

There are no kind people in Hell.

苦 海 没 有 真 人 ，

ku hai mei you zhen ren,

There are no Realised Ones in the Sea of Bitterness.

佛 国 没 有 假 人 。

fo guo mei you jia ren.

There are no false people in the Buddha Land.

用 志 当 人 是 没 有 说 的 、

yong zhi dang ren mei you shuo de,

People using Will to act as human do not discuss,

不 恋 的 ，

bu lian de,

and are without attachment.

你 欺 我 、

ni qi wo,

If you bully "I,"

骂 我 ，

ma wo,

reprimand "I,"

也 是 成 我 。

ye shi cheng wo.

it is also accomplishing "I,"

你 假 、

ni jia,

If you deceive,

你 诈 ，

ni zha,

if you swindle,

也 是 成 我 。

ye shi cheng wo.

it is also accomplishing "I."

就 是 杀 了 我 ，

jiu shi sha le wo,

It is exactly killing "I,"

也 是 成 我 。

ye shi cheng wo.

which is also accomplishing "I."

以 志 当 人 就 是 个 真 。

yi zhi dang ren jiu shi ge zhen.

Using Will to act as human
is exactly being the Truth.

若 是 老 公 公 （翁 父）被 儿 媳 妇 骂 了，

ruo shi lao gong gong (weng fu) bei er xi fu ma le,

It is like the husband's father (father-in-law)
being scolded by the daughter-in-law,

便 该 立 志 说：

bian gai li zhi shuo:

then one must say with resolve,

『你 要 能 骂 动 我，

"ni yao neng ma dong wo,

"If you will be able to stir me by scolding me,

算 我 当 不 起 公 公！』

suan wo dang bu qi gong gong!"

it counts as me not upholding the role as father-in-law!"

能 这 样 定 住 就 是 佛，

neng zhe yang ding zhu jiu shi fo,

If one is able to stabilize like this,
it is like being a Buddha.

是 佛 就 有 神 来 保 护 。

shi fo jiu you shen lai bao hu.

For a Buddha the Spirits will appear for protection.

206

以 意 为 主 就 是 个 乐 ，
yi yi wei zhu jiu shi ge le,
Using Intent as priority is joy.

乐 就 是 神 。
le jiu shi shen.
Joy is exactly Spirit.

各 教 圣 人 ，
ge jiao sheng ren,
Sages and Saints of all religions,

没 有 不 是 以 志 为 主 的 。
mei you bu shi yi zhi wei zhu de.
not one of them did not consider
Will as their priority.

我 听 说 ，
wo ting shuo,
I have heard,

孔 子 在 陈 绝 粮 ，
kong zi zai chen jue liang,
that when Confucius severed from grain
in the country of Chen,[39]

仍 然 是 坦 荡 自 如 ，
reng ran shi tan dang zi ru,
he was still magnanimous and imperturbable,

弦 歌 不 辍 。

xian ge bu chuo.

ceaselessly singing songs accompanied
by stringed instruments.

又 听 说 ,

you ting shuo,

I also have heard

耶 稣 被 钉 十 字 架 ,

ye su bei ding shi zi jia,

that when Jesus was nailed to the cross,

三 日 复 活 仍 救 世 人 。

san ri fu huo reng jiu shi ren.

after three days he was resurrected
and still saved people from this world.

释 迦 佛 当 忍 辱 真 人 时 ,

shi jia fo dang ren ru zhen ren shi,

When Buddha Shakyamuni,
the Realized One, endured humiliation

被 歌 利 王 割 截 肢 体 ,

bei ge li wang ge cai zhi ti,

and had his body and limbs
severed by King Kalabu,[40]

还 说 :

hai shuo:

he still said,

我 成 佛 先 度 你 !

wo cheng fo xian du ni!

"When I become a Buddha,
first, I will deliver you!"

他 们 这 种 精 神 ,

ta men zhe yang jing shen,

This is the kind of consciousness they had,

是 不 是 一 样 呢 ?

shi bu shi yi yang ne?

is it not the same?

所 以 我 说 ,

suo yi wo shuo,

Therefore I say,

各 教 的 形 式 虽 然 不 同 ,

ge jiao de xing shi sui ran bu tong,

although each religion differs in form

可 是 精 神 是 一 样 的 ,

ke shi jing shen shi yi yang de,

their essence and spirit are the same.

若 是 分 门 别 派 就 不 对 啦 !
ruo shi fen men bie pai jiu bu dui la!
It seems that the division into schools and the
differentiation into sects is actually incorrect!

当 今 之 世 ,
dang jin zhi shi,
In today's age,

诸 天 神 佛 ,
zhu tian shen fo,
the Spirits and Buddhas of all Heavens

全 在 人 间 ,
quan zai ren jian,
are wholly amongst the people,

可 并 没 有 投 生 落 凡 。
ke bing mei you tou sheng luo fan.
but they have not reincarnated
and shed the ordinary at all.

夺 谁 的 志 ,
duo shei de zhi,
Whichever Will you seize,

谁 的 灵 就 来 。
shei de ling jiu lai.
the Divinity of that Will at once arrives.

学 那 位 神 佛 ,
xue na wei shen fo,
Whichever Spirit or Buddha you learn from,

那 位 神 佛 的 灵 就 到 。
na wei shen fo de ling jiu dao.
that Divinity of that exact Spirit or Buddha
at once arrives.

学 那 位 圣 贤 ,
xue na wei sheng xian,
Whichever Sage and Saint you learn from,

那 位 圣 贤 就 来 。
na wei sheng xian jiu lai.
that virtuous Sage or Saint at once arrives.

遇 着 什 么 事 ,
yu zhe shen me shi,
The situations you come across

就 学 什 么 人 。
jiu xue shen me ren.
is where you learn from people.

像 摘 (挑 取) 花 样 似 的 ,
xiang ti (tiao qu) hua yang si de,
It is the same as selecting (picking) flowers.

摘一个做一个。

ti yi ge zuo yi ge.

Pick one, arrange one.

孟子说:

Meng Zi shuo:

Mencius says:

『人皆可以为尧舜』,

"ren jie ke yi wei yao shun,"

"All people can become like Emperor Yao and Shun."[41]

就是叫人夺志。

jiu shi jiao ren duo zhi.

It is the same as calling people to seize the Will.

平常人要不夺古人的志,

ping chang ren yao bu duo gu ren de zhi,

Common people will not seize the Will of the ancients.

终久是个平常人。

zhong jiu shi ge ping chang ren.

After all, they are common people.

真到了志界,

zhen dao le zhi jie,

Once truly arrived in the Realm of Will,

半点火气也没有，
ban dian huo qi ye mei you,
the least bit of Fire and Qi does not exist,

只剩真乐啦！
zhi sheng zhen le la!
all that is remaining is true joy!

The mountain summit of will and intent

（十）

Chapter 10

学 道

Xue Dao

The Study
of the Dao

人 的 心 理，

ren de xin li,

Inside people's Hearts,

总 是 好 高，

zong shi hao gao,

there is always fondness of lofty heights,

都 是 爱 好 。

dou shi ai hao.

all of them being desirous of doing better.

哪 知 事 全 糟 在 高 上 、

na zhi shi quan zao zai gao shang,

Beginning to understand matters becomes
completely wretched atop lofty heights,

坏 在 好 上 ，

huai zai hao shang,

spoiling atop that fondness.

好 上 、

hao shang,

Atop fondness

高 处 那 里 有 道 呢 ？

gao chu na li you dao ne?

or lofty heights, where does the Dao still exist?

人 是 正 眼 没 开 ,

ren shi zheng yan mei kai,

People's Upright Eyes have not opened yet.

把 道 看 错 啦 !

ba dao kan cuo la!

They have mistaken the Dao!

别 人 不 做 的 你 去 做 ,

bie ren bu zuo de ni qu zuo,

What other people do not do, you venture to do.

别 人 抛 弃 的 你 捡 来 ,

bie ren pao qi de ni jian lai,

What other people abandon, you pick up.

那 就 是 德 ,

na jiu shi de,

This is the same as Virtue.

也 就 是 道 。

ye jiu shi dao.

It is also the Dao.

像 水 的 就 下 ,

xiang shui de jiu xia,

People who imitate Water lower themselves,

把 一 切 物 全 托 起 来 ，

ba yi qie wu quan tuo qi lai,

supporting all things from underneath,

自 然 归 服 你 ，

zi ran gui fu ni,

naturally obeying you

自 然 服 从 你 ，

zi ran fu cong ni,

and naturally serving you.

这 叫 托 底 。

zhe jiao tuo di.

This is called propping up the bottom.

可 惜 人 都 好 抢 上 ，

ke xi ren dou hao qiang shang,

It is a pity that people are all fond of vying,

不 肯 就 下 ，

bu ken jiu xia,

disapprovingly and unwillingly they lower themselves.

所 以 离 道 远 啦 ！

suo yi li dao yuan la!

This is the reason why this is far removed
from the Dao!

世人都怕水深火热，
shi ren dou pa shui shen huo re,
People of this world are all afraid of the depths
of waters and the heat of fires,

怕死在里面。
pa si zai li mian.
fearing to die within.

岂不知好名的死在名上，
qi bu zhi hao ming de si zai ming shang,
How could they not know that being fond of fame,
one will die atop this fame.

好利的死在利上，
hao li de si zai li shang,
Being fond of gain, one will die atop of gain.

每天都处在水深火热之中，
mei tian dou chu zai shui shen huo re zhi zhong,
Everyday day they are in the depths
of waters and the heat of fires,

自己还不知道呢！
zi ji hai bu zhi dao ne!
but, they themselves are still unknowing!

我讲道，
wo jiang dao,
I explain the Dao:

不要名是『入火不焚』、

bu yao ming shi "ru huo bu fen,"

Not wanting fame is "Entering Fire Without Burning."

不要钱是『入水不溺』。

bu yao qian shi "ru shui bu ni."

not wanting money is "Entering Water Without Drowning."

我学道先学损、

wo xue dao xian xue sun,

When I study the Dao,
I first learn about decrease,

学穷，

xue qiong,

learn about poverty,

别人学高、

bie ren xue gao,

while other people learn about lofty heights,

学讲学问，

xue jiang xue wen,

learn about negotiating and learn about examining,

所以没赶上我。

suo yi mei gan shang wo.

therefore they do not keep up with me.

知 足 才 能 落 底 ，

zhi zu cai neng luo di,

Knowing contentment, you are able
to drop to the bottom.

知 足 才 能 得 道 ，

zhi zu cai neng de dao,[42]

knowing contentment,
then you are able to attain the Dao,

这 是 得 道 的 要 诀 。

zhe shi de dao de yao jue.

This is the essential secret of achieving the Dao.

道 是 天 道 ，

dao shi tian dao,

The Dao is the Heavenly Dao.

人 人 都 有 ，

ren ren dou you,

Every single person has it.

并 没 离 开 人 。

bing mei li kai ren.

It is not at all separated from people.

今 人 为 什 么 没 得 着 呢 ？

jin ren wei shen me mei de zhe ne?

Why do people of today have yet
to attain the Dao?

举例来说，

ju lie lai shuo,

To give an example,

一颗豆子，

yi ke dou zi,

one pearl of a bean,

有了秧必须向上度浆，

you le yang bi xu xiang shang du jiang,

when it sprouts, it must be watered
and nurtured from the top.

把豆粒度成了算。

ba dou li du cheng le suan.[43]

Pouring nutrients and water on the bean
successfully is what counts.

人也有本，

ren ye you ben,

People also have a Root.

常心思自己的本（分），

chang xin si zi ji de ben (fen),

Constantly the Heart ponders
about one's own Root (allotment).

诚心求三个月，

cheng xin qiu san ge yue,

If the sincere Heart seeks for three months,

便 能 得 着 ,
bian neng de zhao,
then it is capable of reaching it.

这 是 我 求 做 活 道 得 着 的 。
zhe shi wo qiu zuo huo dao de zhe de.
This is what I achieved when I sought,
engaged in, and toiled in the Dao.

好 高 是 贪 ,
hao gao shi tan,
Fondness of lofty heights is covetous.

怕 坏 是 粘 ;
pa huai shi zhan;
Being afraid of spoiling is attachment.

好 好 是 孽 ;
hao hao shi nie;
Being fond of goodness is a wrongdoing.

嫌 不 好 是 缺 德 ;
xian bu hao shi que de;
Disliking the no-good is lacking virtue.

不 尽 职 是 丢 天 命 。
bu jin zhi shi diu tian ming.
Not doing one's duty is losing
one's Heavenly Destiny.

只一个好字，
zhi yi ge hao zi,
Just this one word, Goodness,

把英雄豪杰都坑害啦！
ba ying xiong hao lie dou keng hai la!
traps all heroes and brave warriors in the pit!

Nurturing of the inherent seed of the Dao

（十一）

Chapter 11

立 命

Li Ming

The Establishing of Life-Destiny

世 人 都 愿 享 福 ，

shi ren dou yuan xiang fu,

People of this world, all wish to enjoy good fortune.

为 什 么 享 福 的 人 少 、

wei shen me xiang fu de ren shao,

Why are there few people enjoying good fortune

受 苦 的 人 多 呢 ？

shou ku de ren duo ne?

and people who endure suffering are many?

因 为 人 一 不 知 足 、

yin wei ren yi bu zhi zu,

It is because, one, people do not know contentment

二 不 认 命 。

er bu ren ming.

and, two, they do not accept Life-Destiny.

人 要 明 道 ，

ren yao ming dao,

People must grasp the Dao.

有 福 会 享 ，

you fu hui xiang,

If you have good fortune,

you are able to enjoy it.

没 福 也 会 找 。

mei fu ye hui zhao.

If you do not have good fortune,
you are able to find it as well.

看 自 己 不 如 人 ，

kan zhe zi ji bu ru ren,

If you see yourself less than Human,

那 叫 自 欺 ，

na jiao zi qi,

that is called self-bullying.

也 叫 不 知 足 ，

ye jiao bu zhi zu,

It is also called not knowing contentment.

这 种 人 准 苦 。

zhe zhong ren zhun ku.

These types of people are granted Bitterness.

知 足 的 人 天 命 一 定 长 ，

zhi zu de ren tian ming yi ding zhang,

The Heavenly Life-Destiny of people who know
contentment will certainly grow.

情 理 足 道 理 长 ，

qing li zu dao li zhang,

If the Principles of Reason suffice,
then the Principles of the Dao grow.

233

道 理 足 天 理 长，

dao li zu tian li zhang,

If the Principles of the Dao suffice,
then the Heavenly Principles grow.

足 了 就 不 费 力 。

zu le jiu bu fei li.

Once sufficient, then there is no expenditure of vigor.

若 是 做 这 个 想 那 个，

ruo shi zuo zhe ge xiang na ge,

If you do this, but wish for that,

叫 做 漏 气 。

jiao zuo lou qi.

it is called leakage of Qi.

像 气 球 似 的，

xiang qi qiu si de,

Just like the air balloon,

一 漏 气 就 瘪 了 ！

yi lou qi jiu bie le!

once you leak Qi, you will shrivel up!

又 像 蒸 包 子，

you xiang zheng bao zi,

It is also like steaming buns.

一 漏 气 就 生 了 。

yi lou qi jiu sheng le.

Once there is leakage of Qi, they will be uncooked.

所 以 君 子 做 事 不 嫌 事 小 ,

suo yi jun zi zuo shi bu xian shi xiao,

Therefore, when noble people undertake affairs,
they do not complain of minor affairs.

有 十 分 力 量 使 七 分 ,

you shi fen li liang shi qi fen,

If you have ten parts of power, employ seven parts,

又 轻 松 又 愉 快 ,

you qing song you yu kuai,

both relaxed and joyous,

就 是 活 神 仙 。

jiu shi huo shen xian.

this is exactly a Living Spirit Immortal.

一 起 贪 心 ,

yi qi tan xin,

Once one raises a Heart of Greed,

便 落 苦 海 ,

bian luo ku hai,

one then falls into the Sea of Bitterness.

不 论 怎 样 大 富 大 贵 ，

bu lun zen yang da fu da gui,

regardless of how great one's wealth and rank,

也 是 毫 无 乐 趣 。

ye shi hao wu le qu.

it is absolutely without joy.

命 就 是 人 的 本 分 ，

ming jiu shi ren de ben fen,

Life-Destiny is precisely people's duty.

守 住 本 分 就 立 住 了 天 命 。

shou zhu ben fen jiu wei zhu le tian ming.

Safeguarding one's duty is the same
as establishing one's Heavenly Life-Destiny.

天 命 长 ，

tian ming chang,

When one's Heavenly Life-Destiny is great,

名 也 准 大 起 来 。

ming ye zhun da qi lai.

one's reputation is also granted to expand.

会 当 九 个 人 就 得 着 九 条 道 。

hui dang jiu ge ren jiu de zhe jiu tiao dao.

If one is able to act as nine people,
one will obtain the Nine Paths of the Dao.

若 是 不 尽 职 、

ruo shi bu jin zhi,

If one is not fulfilling one's duty,

不 尽 力 、

bu jin li,

not giving one's best,

喜 虚 荣 、

xi xu rong,

delighting in empty honor,[44]

做 假 事 、

zuo jia shi,

dealing with sham affairs,

有 名 无 实 ,

you ming wu shi,

or having fame without reality,

就 立 不 住 命 。

jiu li bu zhu ming.

then one cannot establish Life-Destiny.

道 是 行 的 ,

dao shi xing de,

The Dao is to be cultivated.

德 是 做 的 ,

de shi zuo de,

Virtue is to be acted out.

不 行 没 有 道 ,

bu xing mei you dao,

Without Cultivation there is no Dao.

不 做 没 有 德 。

bu zuo mei you de.

Without action there is no virtue.

上 天 按 天 理 命 名 ,

shang tian an tian li ming ming,

Ascension to Heaven is assigned in accordance
with the Principles of Heaven.

人 要 照 本 分 行 事 ,

ren yao zhao ben fen xing shi,

People must accord with their duty
when undertaking affairs.

就 合 天 道 。

jiu he tian dao.

This is the same as unifying with the Heavenly Dao.

本 着 天 道 所 做 的 就 是 天 德 ,

ben zhe tian dao suo zuo de jiu shi tian de,

Conforming with all doings of the Heavenly Dao
is Heavenly Virtue.

也 就 能 不 思 而 得 。

ye jiu neng bu si er de.

One is also capable to gain without contemplation.

行 道 不 可 出 本 位 ,

xing dao bu ke chu ben wei,

Cultivating the Dao, one must not exit
outside one's Original Position.

若 是 离 开 本 位 ,

ruo shi li kai ben wei,

If one is separated from the Original Position,

不 但 劳 而 无 功 ,

bu dan lao er wu gong,

it is not only toilsome, but also without merit.

反 而 有 过 。

fan er you guo.

On the contrary it is a mistake.

什 么 是 本 位 呢 ?

shen me shi ben wei ne?

What is the Original Position?

就 是 人 的 本 分 ,

jiu shi ren de ben fen,

It is exactly people's duty.

『素位而行』就可以成道。

"su wei er xing" jiu ke yi cheng dao.

"In an Unadorned Position Yet Cultivating,"
then one is able to achieve the Dao.

人要『素位而行』,

ren yao "su wei er xing,"

People need to be "In an Unadorned Position
Yet Cultivating."

做事不出本位,

zuo shi bu chu ben wei,

When dealing with affairs, one does not exit
out of one's Original Position.

说话不出本位,

shuo hua bu chu ben wei,

When speaking, one does not exit
out of one's Original Position.

思想不出本位,

si xiang bu chu ben wei,

When thinking, one does not exit
out of one's Original Position.

才能当体成真。

cai neng dang ti cheng zhen.

Only then can the Body be considered
to be the accomplishment of Truth.

若是生为女身，

ruo shi sheng wei nü shen,

If born as a woman,

羡慕男人，

xian mu nan ren,

she is envious of men.

贫穷人妄想富贵，

pin qiong ren wang xiang fu gui,

If poor, people are wishfully thinking
about wealth and rank,

做这个想那个，

zuo zhe ge xiang na ge,

and are doing this, but contemplating that,

全是出位的人，

quan shi chu wei de ren,

they are all people who will exit out of their position.

怎能成道呢？

zen neng cheng dao ne?

How could one achieve the Dao?

就像梨要成在梨树上，

jiu xiang li yao cheng zai li shu shang,

It is like the pear that must ripen on the pear tree.

不能再杏树上成。

bu neng zai xing shu shang cheng.

It can not ripen on the apricot tree.

八德是八个门,

ba de shi ba ge men,

The Eight Virtues[45] are Eight Gates.

都能进入佛国。

dou neng jin ru fo guo.

All of them enter into the Buddha Land.

不过人应当从那个门进,

bu guo ren ying dang cong na ge men jin,

However, it is only when people ought
to enter from that gate

就由那个门进,

jiu you na ge men jin,

that the one gate is to be followed to enter

这就是『素位而行』的意思。

zhe jiu shi "su wei er xing" de yi si.

and this is the exact meaning of
"In an Unadorned Position Yet Cultivating."

我是由忠、

wo shi you zhong,

I follow loyalty

孝 两 个 门 进 来 的 ，
xiao liang ge men jin lai de,
and filial piety, these two gates,
I entered them through

给 人 放 牛 、
gei ren fang niu,
herding oxen for people

扛 活 （佣 工） 全 部 抱 定 一 个 忠 字 ；
kang huo (yong gong) quan dou bao ding yi ge zhong zi;
and working as a farm laborer (hired laborer),
they all hold fast to the word loyalty.

对 老 人 ，
dui lao ren,
For the elderly

抱 定 一 个 孝 字 ，
bao ding yi ge xiao zi,
holding fast to the words filial piety,

这 是 我 敢 自 信 的 。
zhe shi wo gan zi xin de.
this is what I dare to be self-confident about.

『 命 者 名 也 』，
"ming zhe ming ye,"
"Life-Destiny also defines reputation."

名正，

ming zheng,

If one's fame is upright,

命就正了。

ming jiu zheng le.

it means one's Life-Destiny is also upright.

命正、

ming zheng,

If one's Life-Destiny is upright,

性自然就化啦。

xing zi ran jiu hua la.

then one's Inner Nature naturally transforms.

所以教人最重要的是教性、

suo yi jiao ren zui zhong yao de shi jiao xing,

Therefore, when teaching people, the most
important aspect is to teach about Inner Nature

教命。

jiao ming.

and to teach about Life-Destiny.

True pears

化 性
Hua Xing

The Transformation of Inner Nature

人 落 在 苦 海 里,

ren luo zai ku hai li,

When people fall into the Sea of Bitterness,

要 是 没 有 会 游 泳 的 去 救,

yao shi mei you hui you yong de qu jiu,

if there is no one able to come swimming to their rescue,

自 己 很 难 出 来,

zi ji hen nan chu lai,

they will have a lot of difficulty to make it out
by themselves.

因 此 我 立 志 要 救 人 的 性 命。

yin ci wo li zhi yao jiu ren de xing ming.

For this reason I am determined to save
people's Inner Nature and Life-Destiny.

救 人 的 命 是 一 时 的,

jiu ren de ming shi yi shi de,

Saving people's Life-Destiny is one moment,

还 在 因 果 里;

hai zai yin guo li;

yet they are still inside of Cause and Effect.

救 人 的 性,

jiu ren de xing,

Saving people's Inner Nature

是 永 远 的 ,
shi yong yuan de,
is eternal.

是 一 救 万 古 、
shi yi jiu wan gu,
Once saved for Ten Thousand Ages,[46]

永 断 循 环 。
yong duan xun huan.
it forever cuts off the Cycles.

所 以 救 命 是 有 形 的 ,
suo yi jiu ming shi you xing de,
Therefore, saving Life-Destiny has form.

是 一 时 的 ;
shi yi shi de;
It is one instant.

救 性 是 无 形 的 ,
jiu xing shi wu xing de,
Saving Inner Nature is formless.

是 万 劫 不 朽 的 。
shi wan jie bu xiu de.
It is for Ten Thousand Generations
never decaying.

人 性 被 救 ,

ren xing bei jiu,

If the Human Inner Nature is saved,

如 出 苦 海 ,

ru chu ku hai,

it is as if coming out of the Sea of Bitterness,

如 登 彼 岸 ,

ru deng bi an,

as if stepping on the Other Shore

永 不 坠 落 。

yong bu duo luo.

and never again falling into it.

人 被 事 物 所 迷 ,

ren bei shi wu suo mi,

If people get mislead by objects,

往 往 认 假 为 真 ,

wang wang ren jia wei zhen,

frequently recognizing falsities as truth,

那 叫 看 不 透 。

na jiao kan bu tou.

this is called Seeing Without Clarity.

所 以 才 说 人 不 对 ，

suo yi cai shuo ren bu dui,

By only saying people are incorrect,

和 人 生 气 上 火 。

he ren sheng qi shang huo.

they raise their Qi and flare up Fire towards people.

其 实 是 自 己 看 不 透 ，

qi shi shi zi ji kan bu tou,

In fact, it is oneself who is Seeing Without Clarity.

若 能 把 世 事 看 透 ，

ruo neng ba shi shi kan tou,

If one can see the affairs of this world clearly,

准 会 笑 起 来 ，

zhun hui xiao qi lai,

one will be allowed to raise laughter.

那 能 和 人 生 气 打 架 呢 ？

na neng he ren sheng qi da jia ne?

How could one raise Qi and fight with people?

我 当 初 看 世 上 没 有 一 个 好 人 ，

wo dang chu kan shi shang mei you yi ge hao ren,

When at first I saw that there were
no good people in this world,

我 就 生 气，

wo jiu sheng qi,

I raised Qi

气 得 长 了 十 二 年 疮 痨，

qi de zhang le shi er nian chuang lao,

and this Qi grew chronic ulcers for twelve years,

几 乎 没 把 我 气 死，

ji hu mei ba wo qi si,

almost ending in my death from choking on anger.

直 到 我 三 十 五 岁 那 年 正 月 听 善 书，

zhi dao wo san shi wu nian na nian zheng yue ting shan shu,

When I was about thirty-five years old, in the first lunar
month of that year I heard of a book about merit.

才 知 道 生 气 不 对，

cai zhi dao sheng qi bu dui,

Only then did I know that raising one's Qi was wrong.

对 天 自 责，

dui tian zi ze,

Facing the Heavens, reproving only myself,

我 的 疮 痨 一 夜 功 夫 就 好 了，

wo de chuang lao yi ye gong fu jiu hao le,

my chronic ulcers were fine
after one night of Gong Fu,[47]

立 刻 出 了 地 狱 。

li ke chu le di yu.

immediately bringing me out of hell.

恭 敬 我 的 ,

gong jing wo de,

People respecting "I,"

正 是 害 我 。

zheng shi hai wo.

are truly harming "I."

羞 辱 我 的 ,

xiu ru wo de,

People humiliating "I,"

正 是 成 我 。

zheng shi cheng wo.

are truly accomplishing "I."

假 的 （ 指 财 、 色 、 荣 、 辱 等 。 ）

jia de (zhi cai, se, rong, ru deng.)

The falsities (referring to wealth,
sex, glory, and dishonor, etc.)

来 了 ,

lai le,

When they come,

要 把 它 看 透 ，
yao ba ta kan tou,
one must see clearly through them.

知 道 是 上 天 使 它 来 考 验 我 的 ，
zhi dao shi shang tian shi ta lai kao yan wo de,
One must know that Heavens
let them appear to test "I."

受 辱 受 罪 ，
shou ru shou zui,
Enduring humiliation and enduring hardships

正 是 消 灭 免 难 。
zheng shi xiao mie mian nan.
is truly eradicating disaster and being exempt
from difficulties.

能 知 人 的 性 ，
neng zhi ren de xing,
Only if being able to know
the Inner Nature of Humans,

才 能 认 识 人 ，
cai neng ren shi ren,
is one able to recognize Humans.

能 知 物 的 性 ,
neng zhi wu de xing,
Only if being able to know
the Inner Nature of Objects,

才 会 利 用 物 ,
cai hui li yong wu,
is one able to take advantage of Objects.

这 是 和 天 接 碴 。
zhe shi he tian jie cha.
This is to pursue a conversation with Heaven.

什 么 样 的 人 ,
shen me yang de ren.
The kind of person you are,

就 存 什 么 心 ,
jiu cun shen me xin,
determines what Heart you preserve,

说 什 么 话 ,
shuo shen me hua,
the kind of words you speak,

办 什 么 事 。
ban shen me shi.
and the kinds of affairs you undertake.

你要是看他不对，

ni yao shi kan ta bu dui,

If you consider others incorrect,

是不知他的性，

shi bu zhi ta de xing,

it is because you do not know their Inner Nature.

也就是不明他的道，

ye jiu shi bu ming ta de dao,

It is also that if you do not understand others' Dao,

准被他气着。

zhun bei ta qi zhao.

you are granted to be angered by them.

就像屎壳螂好推粪球、

jiu xiang shi ke lang hao tui fen qiu,

Just like the dung beetle is fond of pushing
the dung ball,

黄皮子（鼬）好吃小鸡，

huang pi zi (you) hao chi xiao ji,

and the yellow mink (weasel)
is fond of eating small chickens,

争贪的人，

zheng tan de ren,

people who are argumentative and greedy,

好 占 便 宜 。

hao zhan pian yi.

are fond of being in advantageous positions.

那 一 界 的 人 ,

na yi jie de ren,

People of that Realm

办 那 一 界 的 事 ,

ban na yi jie de shi,

handle affairs of that Realm.

所 以 说 都 对 。

suo yi shuo dou dui.

Therefore, what is said, is all correct.

我 受 种 种 打 击 ,

wo shou zhong zhong da ji,

I endure all kinds of attacks.

立 志 不 生 气 、

zhi li bu sheng qi,

If you are resolute, you will not raise Qi

不 上 火 ,

bu shang huo,

and Fire will not flare up.

被人讥笑，

bei ren ji xiao,

Even when being ridiculed by people,

也不动性。

ye bu dong xing.

one's Inner Nature is not stirred.

气、火是两个『无常鬼』，

qi huo shi liang ge "wu chang gui,"

Qi and Fire are two "Impermanent Ghosts."

能把它们降伏住，

neng ba ta men xiang fu zhu,

If one can subdue and tame those,

使火变为『金童』、

shi huo bian wei "jin tong,"

the Fire transforms into "the Golden Boy"

气变为『玉女』，

qi bian wei "yu nü,"

and Qi transforms into "the Jade Maiden."

不受它们克，

bu shou ta men ke,

If one is not subjected to their capture,

那 就 是 佛 。
na jiu shi fo.
one is then a Budhha.

逆 来 的 是 德 ,
ni lai de shi de,
Coming through adversities is virtue.

人 需 要 认 识 ,
ren xu yao ren shi,
People need to recognize,

吃 了 亏 不 可 说 ,
chi le kui bu ke shuo,
when suffering losses, do not speak about it.

必 是 欠 他 的 ,
bi shi qian ta de,
Inevitably, when owing others,

从 人 替 你 抱 屈 ,
cong ren ti ni bao qu,
your servants will report your unfair treatment
on your behalf.

你 就 是 长 命 。
ni jiu shi chang ming.
You then enjoy a long life.

若 是 无 故 挨 打 受 气，

ruo shi wu gu ai da shou qi,

If you receive a beating and suffer
wrong without reason,

也 是 自 己 有 罪，

ye shi zi ji you zui,

it also means that your Self is guilty.

受 过 了 算 还 债，

shou guo le suan huan zhai,

Having endured it counts as repaying debts

还 要 感 激 他，

hai yao gan ji ta,

and you still have to be grateful to others.

若 是 没 有 他 打 骂，

ruo shi mei you ta da ma,

If there had not been others beating and scolding,

我 的 罪 何 时 能 了 ？

wo de zui he shi neng liao?

when could my guilt be finished?

我 说 小 人 也 有 好 处，

wo shuo xiao ren ye you hao chu,

I say even lowly people have positives.

是 挤 兑 人 好 的 ，

shi ji dui ren hao de,

People who insult human goodness

从 反 面 帮 助 人 。

cong fan mian bang zhu ren.

help people from the reverse side.

受 了 受 了 ，

shou liao shou liao,

Accept and endure it.

一 受 就 了 。

yi shou jiu liao.

Once accepted it is then ended.

受 罪 了 罪 ，

shou zui liao zui,

Accept suffering and end suffering.

受 苦 了 苦 。

shou ku liao ku.

Accept Bitterness and end Bitterness.

没 孽 不 挨 骂 ，

mei nie bu ai ma,

Without offense, you will not receive a scolding.

没 罪 不 挨 打 。

mei zui bu ai da.

Without guilt, you will not receiving a beating.

逆 事 来 了 ,

ni shi lai le,

Vexatious matters appear

是 给 你 送 德 来 的 ,

shi gei ni song de lai de,

in order to deliver virtue to you.

不 但 忍 受 ,

bu dan ren shou,

Not only endure and accept,

还 要 感 激 他 。

hai yao gan ji ta.

but also be grateful to others.

一 切 事 没 有 不 是 从 因 果 中 来 的 ,

yi qie shi mei you bu shi cong yin guo zhong lai de,

Of all issues there is none that does
not come from Cause and Effect.

逆 事 来 若 能 乐 哈 哈 地 受 过 去 ,

ni shi lai ruo neng le ha ha de shou guo qu,

When vexatious matters arise, if you are able
to endure past them while joyously laughing,

认 为 是 应 该 的 ，

ren wei shi ying gai de,

reckoning that they are a must,

自 然 就 了 啦 。

zi ran jiu liao la.

they will naturally come to an end.

若 是 受 不 了 ，

ruo shi shou bu liao,

If one is unable to endure until the end,

心 里 含 有 怨 气 ，

xin li han you yuan qi,

and if Resentful Qi is contained within the Heart,

这 件 事 虽 然 过 去 ，

zhe jian shi sui ran guo qu,

despite being past this issue,

将 来 必 有 逆 事 重 来 ，

jiang lai bi you ni shi chong lai,

in the future, vexatious matters will certainly re-emerge.

正 因 为 受 而 未 了 的 原 故 。

zheng yin wei shou er wei liao de yuan gu.

The true reason is because suffering
has not been finished yet.

凡 是 对 面 来 的 ,

fan shi dui mian lai de,

Whatever appears right in front of you,

都 是 命 里 有 的 ,

dou shi ming li you de,

all of it exists in your Life-Destiny.

所 以 遇 着 不 如 意 的 事 、

suo yi yu zhe bu ru yi de shi,

Therefore, whatever issues you encounter
that are not as you wish

不 对 头 的 人 ,

bu dui tou de ren,

and people who are incorrect,

要 能 忍 受 。

yao neng ren shou.

you must endure and accept.

孔 子 在 陈 绝 粮 ,

kong zi zai chen jue liang,

When Confucius severed from food
in the country of Chen,

耶 稣 被 钉 十 字 架 ,

ye su bei da shi zi jia,

when Jesus was nailed to the cross,

佛被割截肢体，

fo bei ge jie zhi ti,

and when Buddha's limbs and body
were cut and severed,

都没怨人，

dou mei yuan ren,

none of them had resentment for the people.

那才是真认命。

na cai shi zhen ren ming.

That is truly accepting one's Life-Destiny.

真认命才能成道。

zhen ren ming cai neng cheng dao.

Truly accepting one's Life-Destiny,
one can become the Dao.

人欺人，

ren qi ren,

People deceive people.

天不欺人，

tian bu qi ren,

Heaven does not deceive people.

天加福是逆来的。

tian jia fu shi ni lai de.

Good fortune conferred from Heaven
comes from oppression.

若 是 遇 着 逆 事 ，

ruo shi yu zhe ni shi,

If encountering vexatious matters

自 己 立 不 住 志 ，

zi ji li bu zhu zhi,

and oneself is unable to have resolve,

那 就 半 途 而 废 了 。

nao jiu ban tu er fei le.

that is giving up halfway.

金 刚 是 最 硬 的 东 西 ，

jin gang shi zui ying de dong xi,

Diamond[48] is the hardest substance,

所 以 要 立 金 刚 志 ，

suo yi yao li jin gang zhi,

therefore one must have a Diamond Resolve.

愚 人 受 人 侮 辱 ，

yu ren shou ren wu ru,

Fools have to endure people's
humiliation and insults,

或 被 人 斥 责 ，

huo bei ren chi ze,

or even people's reprimands.

不 以 为 是 加 福 ，
bu yi wei shi jia fu,
If it is not considered conferred good fortune

反 而 生 气 ，
fan er sheng qi,
and, on the contrary, one raises Qi,

是 刚 倒 了 ！
shi gang dao le!
which is firmness[49] toppling!

明 白 人 好 和 愚 人 生 气 ，
ming bai ren hao he yu ren sheng qi,
Bright people are fond of raising Qi with fools,

是 刚 炸 了 ！
shi gang zha le!
which is firmness exploding!

不 倒 不 炸 ，
bu dao bu zha,
Not toppling, not exploding,

才 能 立 住 金 刚 志 。
cai neng li zhu jin gang zhi,
only then is one able to have Diamond Resolve,

『炼 透 人 情 ，
"lian tou ren qing,
"Thorough Refinement of Human Sentiments

就 是 学 问 』。
jiu shi xue wen"
is Knowledge."

要 在 亲 友 中 去 炼 ，
yao zai qin you zhong qu lian,
If you want to refine amidst family and friends,

炼 成 了 就 不 怕 碰 ，
lian cheng le jiu bu pa peng,
once successfully refined,
there is no fear of bumping into people.

像 砖 瓦 似 的 ，
xiang zhuan wa si de,
It is just like bricks and tiles.

炼 透 了 就 坚 固 。
lian tou le jiu jian gu.
Once the thorough refinement
is completed, they are solid.

炼 不 透 的 如 同 砖 坯 子 ，
lian bu tou de ru tong zhuan pi zi,
The refinement not being thorough
is just like bricks being unbaked.

一 见 水 就 化 了 ！

yi jian shui jiu hua le!

Once they come into contact
with water, they at once change!

要 想 明 德 ，

yao xiang ming de,

If you wish for luminous virtue

必 须 性 圆 。

bi xu xing yuan.

your Inner Nature must be well rounded.

要 想 性 圆 ，

yao xiang xing yuan,

If you want your Inner Nature
to be well rounded,

必 须 死 心 。

bi xu si xin.

you must perish the Heart.

能 装 个 活 死 人 ，

neng zhuang ge huo si ren,

If you are able to become a Living Dead

性 就 化 了 。

xing jiu hua le.

your Inner Nature is completely transformed.

舍 钱 不 如 舍 身 ，

she qian bu ru she shen,

Forsaking money is not as good
as forsaking the Body.

舍 身 不 如 舍 心 ，

she shen bu ru she xin,

Forsaking the Body is not as good
as forsaking the Heart.

舍 心 不 如 舍 性 。

she xin bu ru she xing.

Forsaking the Heart is not as good
as forsaking Inner Nature.

人 能 舍 掉 禀 性 ，

ren neng she diao bing xing,

If people can forsake their
Endowed Natural Dispositions

就 算 得 道 。

jiu suan de dao.

it counts as having achieved the Dao.

所 以 我 教 人 化 性 。

suo yi wo jiao ren hua xing.

Therefore, I teach people
to transform their Inner Nature.

是 一 救 万 古 ，
shi yi jiu wan gu,
Once saved, it is for Ten Thousand Ages

性 灵 不 昧 。
xing ling bu mei.
and the Divinity of Inner Nature
will not be obscured.

Eradication of disaster through humiliation and hardship

275

Notes

1   Despite being borrowed from Christian terminology, the authors decided "Hell" would be the most accessible term to Western readers. It could be alternatively rendered as "the underworlds."

2   *Raising Qi* denotes to get agitated and vexed. *Flaring Up Fire* symbolizes anger or even wrath, in the most negative sense of emotions.

3   *Subduing the* [Red] *Dragon and Taming the* [White] *Tiger* is terminology borrowed from Internal Alchemy. "Subduing the Red Dragon" and "Taming the White Tiger" stands for the stopping of the menses and seminal emissions respectively.

4   *Safeguarding bounds* also implies the upkeep of one's duties.

5   *Fire* (fits of temper) cannot be contained, as it surges and expresses itself outwardly, whereas *Qi* manifests inwardly unnoticeable to the outside. Both, Fire and Qi, are reflections of an imbalanced state and carry negative connotations.

6   *The Seven Places of the Heart's Lantern* [qi chu xin deng 七处心灯] are synonymous to the Seven Chakras [mai lun 脉轮]. It is the goal of cultivators to open these Seven

Places, so as to make the mental state [shen si 神思] radiate and shine similar to a lantern. The term points to the Original Truth of the soul, the psyche and the spirit [xin ling 心灵], as well as its original state. A Heart endowed with the four manners of divine benevolence, righteousness, etiquette and wisdom is also known by the name of the "Heart of Original Goodness" [ben shan zhi xin 本善之心], the "Heart of Sincerity" [cheng xin 诚心], the "Heart of Kindness" [liang xin 良心] and the "Heart of Benevolence" [ren xin 仁心].

Xing De annotates that the "Seven Places of the Heart's Lantern" are seven methods to let go of attachment, but even one is enough.

7   In this instance, "Yin" does not denote something desirable, but something negative.

8   *The Five Elements* is the most widespread translation for the term "Wu Xing" [五行], however the word "Phase" reflects the meaning of "Xing" [行] much closer, since "Xing" [行] refers to "Five Movements" or "Five Ways of Moving through the World." Dr Henry McCann considers the translation "Five Elements" to be one of the biggest problems in Chinese medicine, since it confuses readers as to the real importance of its intended meaning.

9   *Suffer from bullying* in Chinese literally is described as receiving or being subjected to [other people's negative] Qi.

10 *Tai Shang* is the abbreviated honorific title for Tai Shang Lao Jun [太上老君]. He is also the deified form of Lao Zi, author of the *Scripture of Purity and Tranquility* [qing jing jing 清静经] and the famous *Dao De Jing* [道德经] and therefore addressed by the venerable appellation of Dao De Tian Zun [道德天尊]. In the Daoist pantheon he is ranked as one of the three highest Gods, referred to as the Three Pure Ones [san qing 三清]; Yuan Shi Tian Zun [元始天尊], Ling Bao Tian Zun [灵宝天尊] and Dao De Tian Zun [道德天尊].

11 *Fortune and misfortune know no doors, they are invited in* would be an alternative, less literal interpretation of this expression.

12 The word-for-word transliteration of *vanity* in Chinese is "empty honor" or "empty glory."

13 *Cause and Effect* is identical to karma. The Chinese term for karma is made up of of two words, namely "cause" or "reason," and "result" or "consequence."

14 The *spirit of justice* translated literally from the Chinese means "Dutiful Qi" or "Righteous Qi."

15 *Dying within the Five Elements* is representative of being stuck in the karmic cycle of life and death, instead of breaking free and "Dying outside the Five Elements." Arriving and reaching the "Outside of the Five Elements"

is the equivalent of immortality. The normal cycle is as follows:

道生一，一生二，二生三，三生万物。

The Dao gives birth to One,
One gives birth to Two,
Two gives birth to Three,
Three gives birth to the Ten Thousand Things.

Once you return to the Dao or the "Boundless Infinite" [wu ji 无极] the Five Elements no longer exist.

16 *Heaven's Natural Order* comprises several concepts such as the right time, the course of time, destiny and timely opportunities. In the widest sense it is acting according to the "Heavenly Timing" and therefore in accord with the Dao.

17 "I" is interchangeable with "Self" and "Ego."

18 Xing De explicates that the three divisions refer to the three realms of desire [yu jie 欲界], form [se 色] and formlessness [wu se 无色], as well as the three realms of Heaven, Earth and Humans.

19 *A Hundred Officials* simply signifies officials of all ranks and descriptions.

20 Mencius is a a strong advocate of the goodness of Human Nature. In reply to Gao Zi who is quoted shortly thereafter he resorts to the same analogy of water to make his point:

水信无分于东西。无分于上下乎？人性之善也，猶水之就下也。人无有不善，水无有不下。今夫水，搏而跃之，可使过颡；激而行之，可使在山。是岂水之性哉？其势则然也。人之可使为不善，其性亦犹是也。

Water does not at random differentiate into [flowing] *east or west. Would it not be differentiated into* [flowing] *above and below? Human Nature is kind-hearted just as water* [flows] *exactly downwards. There is no human without goodness, just as there is no water that does not flow downwards.*

Today laboring the water, pounce it and it will leap up, it could go past the forehead; swash it, it will travel; it could be made to be atop a mountain. How could this be due to the water's nature? It is the force that makes it so. Humans could be sent into evilness, their nature is also [dealt] *in a similar way.*

21 Xun Zi lived after Mencius in a time of war and turmoil and was an equally dedicated adherent of Confucianism. His dictum was that humans are evil by nature [xing e lun 性恶论], thus his standpoint was at the complete other side of the spectrum compared to Mencius. The full paragraph from the book, bearing the same title *Xun Zi* [荀子] is replicated below:

人之性恶，其善者伪也。今人之性，生而有
好利焉，顺是，故争夺生而辞让亡焉；生而
有疾恶焉，顺是，故残贼生而忠信亡焉；生而
有耳目之欲，有好声色焉，顺是，故淫乱生
而礼义文理亡焉。然则从人之性，顺人之
情，必出于争夺，合于犯分乱理，而归于
暴。故必将有师法之化，礼义之道，然后出
于辞让，合于文理，而归于治。用此观之，
人之性恶明矣，其善者伪也。

*Human Nature is evil; and its goodness is false and
fabricated. Today as for Human Nature, when born
it is also fond of gain. Following along* [with these
indulgences] *is the reason for contention coming into
existence and thus yielding and allowance perishing.*

Born with hate and wickedness, following along [these
sentiments] *is the reason for savage banditry coming
into existence and thus faith and honesty perishing.*

*Born with the desire of ears and eyes, they are fond of
sounds and colors. Following along* [with these desires]
*is the reason for promiscuity coming into existence and
thus etiquette, righteousness, refinedness and reason
perish.*

*That being so, following Human Nature, and
submitting to human sentiments, it certainly will come
out in the form of contention, uniting* [humans] *in
violation of their duties and disorderly reasoning,
as well as a return to violence.*

*That is the reason why there must inevitably be
transformations through the masters' laws and the*

Dao of etiquette and righteousness. Afterwards it will come out in the form of yielding and allowance, uniting [humans] *in refinedness and reason, as well as a return to governance.*

Using this observation, Human Nature is clearly evil, and its goodness is false and fabricated.

22 Gao Zi, a contemporary of Mencius, was a Chinese philosopher who lived during the Warring States Period. Gao Zi firmly believed that education, teaching and direction would determine Human Nature. This is exemplified by a famous Chinese proverb appearing in the *Three Character Classic:*

玉 不 琢 不 成 器 。

If Jade is not cut and polished,
it will not turn into a useful utensil.

23 *Perhaps to the East, perhaps to the West* is an abbreviated quote by Gao Zi that follows below in its entirety. Gao Zi, a contemporary of Mencius, was a Chinese philosopher who lived during the Warring States Period:

性 犹 湍 水 也 ， 决 诸 东 方 则 东 流 ， 决 诸 西 方 则 西 流 。 人 性 之 无 分 于 善 不 善 也 ， 犹 水 之 无 分 于 东 西 也 。

Human Nature resembles rushing water. Burst it open in the east, and it will flow to the east; burst it open in the west, and it will flow to the west.

*Human Nature is not differentiated into good and evil,
in the same way as water is not differentiated into east
and west.*

24 The original text has 愁 [chou] "worries," most likely a
copy mistake.

25 *To work for no reward* also carries the meaning of doing
one's utmost duty.

26 The *Other Shore* depicts the Buddhist concept of Paramita,
a Sanskrit term for perfection, perfect realization, and
reaching beyond.

27 *Xing* [性]and *Ming* [命] are very often paired with each
other and appear as combination. The most common
translation for this evasive term is "Inner Nature" or
"Inner Character and Life-Destiny." *Inner Nature*
encompasses concepts such as attitudes and dispositions,
as well as internal virtues and the internal cultivation
refinement. In Daoism there are specific "Inner Nature
Skill" [xing gong 性功] scriptures and "Life-Destiny
Skill" [ming gong 命功] scriptures. The *The Forty-Nine
Barriers* is a prime example for an "Inner Nature Skill"
scripture. It describes how to refine and forge one's
character traits. It does not, however, explicate how to
transform the physical body, which falls into the domain
of the "Life-Destiny Skill" [ming gong 命功].

28 *River to Hell* [nai he 奈河] is both a Chinese pun and transliteration of the Sanskrit *Naraka* for "Hell," or "Purgatory." It is the river which all souls must cross.

29 *The Yellow Springs* are a synonym for the underworlds.

30 *The Flowers of Heaven and the Wines of Earth* is an idiom for sensual pleasures and debauchery, namely sex and alcohol.

31 *Non-Hearted Humans* carries positive meaning and should not be misread as "heartlessness." In Daoism there is a saying:

人心不死，道心不生。

If the Human Heart does not perish,
the Heart of the Dao cannot be born.

32 An equally valid take on this sentence would be: People of the Realm of the Body only know how to make plans for their bodies.

33 *The Cycle* refers to "Samsara" or the "Wheel of Life."

34 *Non-action* [wu wei] is a central and fundamental concept in Daoism. It describes and illustrates non-action as lacking ownership and attachment to results. It implies that non-action is actually acting spontaneously in accordance with the cycles of the universe, making human deeds the manifestation of the actions of the universe itself.

35 *The Six Paths of the Wheel of Life* are the six realms of
    existence, in which all sentient beings are caught in the
    cycle of Samsara, the cycle of life and death. These realms
    are also commonly translated as the "Six Realms of Karmic
    Rebirth." This cycle repeats itself over countless ages,
    unless one is able to break free from the transmigration
    and reach enlightenment. Depending on one's action
    during one's life one will be reborn in a higher or lower
    realm. Karma and karmic retribution plays a major role
    in this concept. The lower three realms are considered
    evil or bad, whereas the three higher realms are regarded
    as good outcomes.

    The six realms starting from the lowest and worst
    realm are "Hell" [di yu dao 地狱道], "Hungry Ghost"
    [e gui dao 饿鬼道], "Livestock" [chu sheng dao 畜生道],
    Asura [a xiu luo dao 阿修罗道], Humans [ren dao 人道],
    and Deva [tian dao 天道]. It is a misconception to believe
    that the highest realm of heavenly beings is the most
    desirable existence. Although the deva hold god-like
    powers, reigning over celestial kingdoms and living in
    delight and splendor, their authority and powers blind
    them to the world of suffering and fill them with pride.
    It is said that their pleasure is the greatest, so too is their
    misery. It is worth taking note that only humans can make
    progress towards spiritual growth and enlightenment.
    Being born into the human realm is seen as rare, precious
    and fortuitous opportunity. Daoism lays stress on the
    uniqueness of being granted a human life:

一生成仙成佛。

There is only one life to become an Immortal,
to become a Buddha.

To sum it up all six paths are equally part of the cycle of life and death, characterized by suffering and an impermanent existence. Only after the attainment of enlightenment is it possible to obtain permanence in existence. Being within the wheel of karmic rebirth means being subjected to death regardless of which realm one is dwelling in.

36 *The Ruined Star* is a term borrowed from Chinese divination insinuating ill-fate.

37 *The Eye of the Heart* is a more poetic term for conscience, tolerance, consideration and thoughtfulness.

38 Xing De expounds that the "Seed" comprises the theory of the Birth of Yang [yang sheng 阳生], the concept of the seed to become an immortal or Buddha [xian fo zhong zi 仙佛种子], as well as the seed of demonic nature [gui xing 魔性].

39 The *country of Chen* was a vassal state of China in the Zhou Dynasty in today's Henan province.

40 *King Kalabu* is a mythical figure appearing in the
    Khantivadi Jataka. In the story King Kalabu becomes
    outraged upon hearing about his queen being in company
    of a hermit. Some sources claim that it is the superior
    calmness of the ascetic that causes King Kalabu's anger
    to grow out of proportion. In other words, it is the king's
    inability to understand and believe in inner mastery and
    peace that is the reason for his agitation. To be faced with
    silence is to be forced to look inward. The King in an
    attempt to test the ascetic's level of forbearance tortures
    him with whiplashes and ultimately chops his hands and
    legs off. As the ascetic unflinchingly and unswervingly
    upholds his composure and degree of tolerance King
    Kalabu storms off and is struck by lightning shortly
    thereafter.

41 Emperor Yao and Shun were legendary rulers of China and
    sage-kings who lived and ruled more than four thousand
    years ago.

42 Xing De comments that "attaining the Dao" [de dao 得
    道] should be read as "entering the Dao" [jin dao 近道].

43 The sentence should be deciphered as "Let the bean pass
    through its preconceived plan."

44 *Empty honor* is an alternative translation for vanity.

45 The *Eight Virtues* are the eight Confucianist values
and pillars of "respect for one's parents" [xiao 孝],
"brotherhood" [ti 悌], "loyalty" [zhong 忠], "faith"
[xin 信], "propriety" [li 礼], "chivalry" [yi 仪],
"incorruptibility" [lian 廉] and "humility" [chi 耻].

46 *The Ten Thousand Ages* signify eternity.

47 *Gong Fu* does not as commonly believed draw a reference
to Kung Fu and the martial arts associated with it, but it
represent a high skillset. The character for Gong [功] is
composed of two radicals; the former radical [gong 工]
lends its phonetic sound to the word, meaning "work,"
and the latter radical [li 力], depicting power or strength.
Therefore in order to obtain a high skill one must put in
effort, hard work, and strength. To sum it up in the to-the-
point words of Daoist Xing De, "Sweat plus time equals
Gong [功]."

48 *Diamond* [jin gang 金刚] interestingly incorporates the
meaning of the Sanskrit word "Vajra," a thunderbolt and
mythical weapon symbolizing supreme indestructibility
and knowledge in Hinduism and Buddhism.

49 *Firmness* [gang 刚] makes up one part of the word for
diamond [jin gang 金刚] in Chinese, literally translating
as the "Golden Firmness." This firmness could be seen
as a cross-reference to the previously mentioned diamond.

About the Translators

Johan Hausen originally comes from a martial arts background. He holds a second Dan black belt in Tae Kwon Do and competed internationally. He has continued with numerous fighting skills and

longevity techniques for more than twenty years. Through his martial arts adventures he ended up in China's Shaolin Temple and the Wudang Mountain Range for more than four years, where he embarked on a unique journey into the spiritual world of Daoism. Since each combat system is inherently equipped with healing practices, Johan became driven by the possibilities to help people and alleviate suffering.

Johan divides his time between New Zealand, where he practices as a licensed and registered acupuncturist, and China, where he cultivates and facilitates programs at Five Immortals Temple as translator.

Jonas Todd Akers has sought the Way since his early youth. His areas of focus include internal alchemy, movement consciousness, the body-mind connection, spirit cultivation, Qi Gong, Tai Ji and Gongfu.  Despite the onset of a painful neuromuscular disorder known as fibromyalgia at age 23, through diligent study and training he has come to insightful understandings and perspectives on how the process of healing the body, the mind, and the spirit can be achieved for those who truly seek it.